PELICAN BOOKS

Lives of the Great Composers

VOLUME I

(A90)

PELICAN BOOKS

LIVES OF THE GREAT COMPOSERS

I

FROM BYRD TO MOZART AND HAYDN
THE CLASSICS

BACH by W. R. Anderson
BYRD by Richard R. Terry
GLUCK by Martin Du P. Cooper
HANDEL by W. McNaught
HADYN by Dyneley Hussey
MOZART by Dyneley Hussey
PALESTRINA by Richard R. Terry
PURCELL by Ralph Hill
THE SCARLATTIS by Frank Howes

edited by A. L. Bacharach

PUBLISHED BY
PENGUIN BOOKS
WEST DRAYTON MIDDLESEX ENGLAND
245 FIFTH AVENUE NEW YORK U.S.A.

First Published 1935
Published in Pelican Books 1942
Reprinted NOVEMBER 1943
Reprinted NOVEMBER 1947

MADE AND PRINTED IN GREAT BRITAIN
FOR PENGUIN BOOKS LTD., BY WYMAN & SONS LIMITED,
LONDON, FAKENHAM AND READING

EDITOR'S PREFACE

This book and its two companions are about the lives of composers, not about their compositions—a ridiculous division of the indivisible, you may well observe. As reasonably attempt to write a life of Shakespeare and leave out the plays or of Dalton and leave out the atomic theory. Be that as it may, we have attempted to show you the man, explained, if you will, by his creative work, where that has been necessary and possible, rather than the work explained by the man.

In the first volume are gathered together biographies of men who lived in the sixteenth, seventeenth and eighteenth centuries, from Palestrina, who was born in 1525 or 1526, to Haydn, who lived longer than most of our subjects and by dying in 1809—at the good age of 77—carried over the pre-classical and classical period of music into the nineteenth century. The artificiality of a purely arbitrary division into three volumes—as of all such divisions in a living and developing art—is emphatically brought home to us when we recall that Haydn was already eighteen years old in the year of Bach's death, and yet he died only four years before the birth of Verdi and Wagner, both of whom are subjects of biographies in the third volume!

The second volume has been called—for want of a better description—'Beethoven and the Romantics,' a title that, admittedly, begs more questions than it answers. For this title the Editor takes full responsibility and all the blame; the contributors are entirely innocent. In years, the volume covers a much shorter time than does volume one, but not by any means a less pregnant period. From the birth of Beethoven in 1770 to the death of Liszt in 1886, music had undergone changes and developments that must be heard to be believed.

Volume three, 'Brahms, Wagner and their Contemporaries,' carries us from 1813 to the death of Elgar in 1934, covering in years a period very little longer than that of volume two. With perhaps the exception of Debussy, who was in more ways than one 'an end in himself,' the composers included in this volume can claim to have been consolidating and exploiting the advances made by their romantic predecessors rather than breaking lances and idols. It is strange to read to-day of the wild controversies that ranged round the music-dramas of Richard Wagner in a world that knew Berlioz and Liszt, to say nothing of the later Beethoven and the early Verdi.

Nevertheless, the distribution of our subjects between volumes two and three is one that the Editor, for his part, while taking full responsibility, does not really attempt to justify on grounds of logic, aesthetics, or history. And to those who suggest that it is absurd to place Moussorgsky and Liszt in Volume Two, while Tchaikovsky and Wagner find places in Volume Three, the Editor would merely ask, in the words of a famous contemporary, 'What would *you* do?'

A. L. B.

CONTENTS

JOHANN SEBASTIAN BACH

BORN 21 March 1685   DIED 28 July 1750

By W. R. Anderson

The Bach Family Tree

Hail to the Bachs, surely the grandest of all musical tribes!
Their genealogy you can see, for the most part, in Grove's
Dictionary of Music and Musicians: it goes back to about
1560, and after Johann Sebastian the Great, our present
hero (1685-1750), who comes about mid-way, the line tails
off with an amazing number of 'Johann Something-or-
others,' in a curious way which was not fully set forth
until Professor Sanford Terry, the distinguished historian and
Bach-detective, demonstrated it in his *Bach: the Historical
Approach* (Oxford University Press, 1930). To this, with
Professor Terry's numerous other illuminations of the subject,
anyone who writes about Bach in the slightest way must be
deeply indebted. It used to be thought that the last of the
Bachs died about the mid-nineteenth century, but it is now
clear that the tribe did not die out until 1871, fifty-two
descendants having covered the four generations. It is curious
to find that, of the sixteen children of J. S. B. who themselves
ad issue, only one took the lineage past 1818; and when we
come to that son's children, again a solitary member carried
on the good work; and, most surprising of all, not one of
the four children of this last productive Bach (who, like J. S.,
was twice married) had any issue at all. What a large decline
from the greatest Bach, who had a round score of children!
Various modern Bachs up and down Europe have claimed
to be descended from the illustrious family, but Professor

9

Terry will have none of them. After nearly three solid centuries of musical Bachs, marvellously inter-married, the last expired in 1871 : the great line is extinct.

'Cultivating their Garden'

How could Johann Sebastian help being musical?   His father, like *his* father before him, handed down the tradition of music making—fiddling and organ playing chiefly—and of early marrying and big-family rearing. Johann Sebastian, the youngest of eight children, in his turn carried on the traditions, outdoing most of his ancestors with those twenty children ('an habitual parent,' as the schoolboy's essay has it), and all of them, by becoming the greatest musician of the race : one of the greatest the world has ever heard.

The Bachs lived and worked and died in one corner of the world. Other musicians travelled widely, some as juvenile prodigies, such as Mozart and Liszt, some to get experience (like Handel) ; but the Bachs tended their garden away in those small Thuringian states (the capital is now Weimar, a city known to most people by its association with Liszt and Wagner), and cared little for the world without. Johann Sebastian moved about only as his professional advancement dictated. He never even met Handel. What fruitful impregnation might have come about, in contrast to Handel's who settled among us, if Bach had lived here for even a few years. Yet I wonder whether we should have rightly appreciated him. Would not Handel have taken our national fancy more, as he did until quite recently, when Bach began to forge ahead? But let us not set one against the other ! If Bach *had* come amongst us, it would have been to enter our age of Pope and Swift, of John Wesley's evangelism, of elements so diverse, yet connected, as the beginning of the National Debt, too much port-drinking, chimney-boys, and the South Sea Bubble. Though our wars were less mercilessly concentrated than Germany's, we had the sad Scots stories of the '15 and the '45; whilst James II,

William and Mary, Anne, and the first two Georges went their apparently glorious way.

Bach is not one of history's picturesque figures. He did not starve in a garret, nor did he sensationally triumph in conflict with vicious enemies. He did not leave us sheaves of those exciting, self-revealing letters which often reveal something very different when we hear the other correspondent's side of the case; nor did he have any love affairs that he wanted either to hide or flaunt. He was a sober, respectable townsman, 'our worthy organist Mr. Bach'—worthy, as most of his church employers considered, of no star's stipend, but only of the average decent pay—and it was often then, as now, poor enough pay for a fair workman, never mind a genius.

Though few musicians' lives are outwardly more clearly accounted for than Bach's, as far as the documents go, we have never got to know a great deal about his inner life. We cannot well suspect the existence of hidden aspects of the man's activities; but the documents, though they tell us the details of his work and movements, do not show us his entire life. One thing any picture of Bach makes clear —his force of character. Mark that jaw, and the prominent, slightly bent nose! He had a temper, too, that both he and his masters had to wrestle with more than once.

Modern criticism looks below the surface. It may be argued that the rich emotional side of the nature of a great composer is at odds with a period apparently so little congenial to it as that in which Bach lived. It is a mistake to regard Bach's music as unemotional; even if he never gushed, he was not the cool formalist that he used to be thought. Admittedly, the religious life in which he lived and worked was not in itself most likely to produce music highly charged with emotion or mysticism: yet such qualities dwell in much that he wrote. But it is difficult, I think, to find any great conflict or repression in Bach, though it is well to remember how little we really know of his inner life. When he was asked for particulars of himself, for a book of biographies (his later years saw the beginning of a good deal of history-writing, dictionary-making, kindred activities—even a little musical journalism), he did not furnish them. Well for me that I did not have to write this section in J. S. B.'s day! Mr. Ernest Newman, musing on Bach's life in Leipzig, reminds us that Goethe, who knew it very soon after Bach's time, called the city 'a little Paris.' What part, if any, of this city of gaiety and wit could have known J. S. Bach? The documents tell us almost nothing. Have they all disappeared, wonders Mr. Newman, or is it just that Bach was so busy working and running his family that he had no other life at all?

Background

In an age of strife, he sought the quiet mind. And what an age that was, with its monstrous tale of wars that shook Bach's native land; the wastage after the Thirty Years' War, the French encroachments, the extraordinary number of petty States, with their mercenary bishops and princelings. The noble, romantic Rhine castles need to be viewed with Feuchtwanger's *Jew Süss* in mind! Another useful book, that describes the literature of the time against the background of politics and social life, is W. H. Bruford's *Germany in the Eighteenth Century* (Cambridge University Press). Oudenarde, Malplaquet, Ramillies—we remember Marlborough's battles in the War of the Spanish succession, so profitless for Germany: these were going on while young Bach was growing to manhood; and the kingdom of Prussia arose from the Electorate of Brandenburg (a name which every Bach-lover associates with the famous set of concertos) when he was sixteen. His musical contemporaries, besides Handel, were the violin master Tartini, and Pergolesi, with the two Scarlattis and Corelli, in Italy, Couperin (of whom a word later) and the opera-composer Rameau, in France, our Purcell (and for a short time Arne). Wren was at work on our churches, Watteau, Hogarth and Chardin were great names in the graphic arts. Besides Pope and Swift, there was Dryden, who died when Bach was fifteen. Voltaire, Rousseau and Samuel Johnson were firing their intellectual guns, Goldsmith was growing up in Bach's later years. Fielding was shaping the novel, Hume and Gray, Steele and Addison —a wonderful band—were at work. Newton, Leibnitz and Linnæus glorified science, and Captain Cook was gaining youthful experience, while the inventive Benjamin Franklin enlivened all that he touched, and the Nieu Amsterdam of his day had become New York a few years before Bach was born.

Bach's personal background was filled, as we noted, with town-musicians: two 'grands' in the Bach parentage took him straight to old Veit, the miller guitar-player. A grandson of Veit's was Johann Sebastian's grandfather. J. S.'s father, a viola player, had come to live at Eisenach (which you will find about, roughly, the centre of Germany, in Thuringia a home of mediæval Minstrelsy) some fourteen years before Johann Sebastian was born, on 21st March, 1685. He went through the ordinary school life (which began, in Spartan fashion, at 6 a.m. in summer and 7 the rest of the year). He was absent a good deal—presumably through childish illnesses. When he was nine, his mother died, and his father outlived her but a year. So the eldest brother took charge of the younger orphans. This brother, Johann Christoph, was then aged twenty-four, and married. He was an able organist, a pupil of the famous Pachelbel. He lived at Ohrdruf, a small town thirty miles from Eisenach, and here the children found a new home, and continued their studies—in music, with the brother, and in other subjects at the local *Gymnasium*, which was a considerable advance upon that at Eisenach, for an enlightened Duke had started a new system of education, including even object lessons; so Bach learned something of the wider world around him. Apart from this there was little frippery. The curriculum looked well after religious and classical knowledge, and after music, too, for Bach got an average of nearly an hour a day at it.

Religious studies early gripped his mind, and later in life he got together a good library of theology.

Self-Help

Few anecdotes light up the character of the lad; one, told of him at this time, attests the truth which the slightest examination of his manuscripts demonstrates—that he was a great self-helper and self-instructor, and a hard worker. Indeed, his only explanation, when asked the secret of his success, was that he 'worked hard.' He realised, like a lad of good sense, that he could best learn by finding out how others had gone about the fascinating business of composition: he copied out, then and often afterwards, the works of composers whom he admired. Sometimes he rearranged pieces by them for different combinations of instruments, as in the matter of the Vivaldi concertos we hear at the 'Proms.' One of the few Bach anecdotes tells how, when his brother had for some reason refused him access to some sheets of music which he wished to copy, and which were locked up in a cupboard with some kind of open-work front, he contrived to withdraw the sheets, and during half a year assiduously copied them, bit by bit, putting them back every day.

In general studies Johann was a lively-minded learner who seems to have made the most of his opportunities. Happily was it so, for he was not able to go forward to a university: the need to make an early living was too clear.

Going Through the Mill

Some of the best composers began as choirboys. It is, indeed, an excellent start for a musician, thus at once to make music (with others) with the most natural of all instruments, and to get to know something of the great store of choral treasures. At fifteen (in 1700) young Sebastian had to fend for himself. With a friend he got a post as choirboy at the convent of St. Michael at Lüneburg, a town about two hundred miles off, where some of the music by earlier Bachs was well known and appreciated. Besides developing his knowledge of church music, he heard, at another church, a distinguished organist, Böhm, who, it would seem, fired him with the desire to hear as many fine organists as he could: a passion that many young church musicians have felt; but no ordinary, keen student it was who hearkened to Böhm at Lüneberg, and who (perhaps stirred by hearing Böhm speak of his master) soon began to go over to Hamburg to hear that aged master, Reinken, at St. Katharine's, then regarded by many as the doyen of organists. There was no question, for a poor choirboy, of transport other than his legs. Thirty miles is a tidy tramp, and many a time Bach performed it, as well as another journey, to Celle, sixty miles off, where a different sort of stimulating experience was to be had, in hearing the Court band, composed of French players, in French music. Later we find Bach writing some 'French Suites,' which form an excellent introduction to his music for pianists. He must have got many quite fresh ideas from this Celle band, for the light, bright style of Couperin, then the reigning French master, was very different from that of most of the solid native organist-composers that Bach so far knew—though Bach's first hero, Böhm, admired and reflected the French quality, as well as that of the German classics, Pachelbel, Buxtehude, Schütz and others. It was fashionable for the nobility to patronise French arts. Their patronage was too often merely imitative, not creative, and held up the progress of German art. That was only one of the stumbling-blocks in the path of an artist in that century. Another was that professional people were not in general regarded as of importance. Yet this system of little princedoms, repugnant though it is to democratic ideas, had one good result, in that, as these rulers vied with each other in the quality of their musical appointments, they provided a great deal of work for musicians, and gave composers the means not only of getting a living, but of experimenting in composition and hearing their works performed. The system created a lively, if limited, musical life, and there are some who wish we could return to an enlightened modification of it to-day. In America, during the boom years before the war, there was a reflection of it, in the patronage of orchestras by millionaires.

A Stroke of Luck

To this choirboy-pilgrimage period belongs the second of the classic Bach anecdotes. One day, the story goes, he had, upon one of his tramps, come to rest outside an inn, wishing he could enter and take his ease, but without the money to do so. Someone must have seen the weary lad, for a window opened for an instant, and a couple of fish-heads were thrown out: not, apparently, either a golden or a gracious gift; but Bach was not too proud to pick them up, and inside each he found a coin—a ducat, it is generally denominated: presumably, then, worth about nine shillings.

It was natural that, hearing the organ performances of fine players, Bach should want to write music 'like that,' and he began at Lüneburg to write whatever occurred to him—chiefly variations upon hymn tunes—'chorale partitas,' as we call them: most of them very much trial-shots; one or two very much more. Just before he died he was writing music of this type, though more concentrated and, naturally, richer and deeper; but even his early, if not quite his earliest, treatment of the beloved German hymns, or chorales, shows that he was the marked master of this form. No one gets to the heart of Bach who does not know his 'chorale preludes'; and anyone who can hear them should try first to get the words, because Bach uses many subtly beautiful devices to give point and poignancy to them: one little figure will stand, in his mind, for the idea of grief, another for aspiration, and so forth: a trace of the 'programme music' spirit, in fact. Some of these chorale preludes, by the way, have been made available in orchestral arrangements on gramophone records (notably, by the Philadelphia Orchestra). Impressive as these are, the enthusiast may be recommended not to miss hearing these, and as many others as he can, played by one of our many splendid organists upon the instrument for which they were thought out, and which most truly sets forth their nature.

But a choirboy's voice, at its best one of the purest of musical pleasures, soon vanishes. Before he was eighteen he was, as it were, a supernumerary, getting useful experience outside the actual singing work—in accompanying, helping the choirmaster, and so on; but he had to look out for a job, and after an unsuccessful application for an organist's place, and a few months in 1703 in a ducal band at Weimar, he got the post of organist and choirmaster at a new church at Arnstadt, where his salary, including an allowance for board and lodging, was apparently a little over eight guineas a year; but Otto Deutsch estimates that 'the purchasing power of the unit has sunk to one-seventh of what it was 150 years ago'; so Bach was not so badly off, in a frugal day, with the equivalent of about sixty pounds per annum of present-day money.

Up to now he had not had access to any really good organ. Here at Arnstadt was that supreme joy of the organist, a new instrument (even if he had missed the final delight of drawing up its specification himself: he was, like most players, keen on that sort of thing); and Bach was a born organist. He could expand at Arnstadt, for his church duties did not claim him all day and every day: expand not, perhaps, in ways that every young composer would have thought the most exciting, for his was (and always was to be) the life of a quiet-minded man, not seeking wide publicity or gadding about the world. Yet Arnstadt, by allowing him to develop his peculiar greatness as a composer for the organ and the church, provided, at the right time, the most fruitful soil.

He began to branch out, with the first of those cantatas of which he was to leave us nearly three hundred, and with more elaborate organ pieces: some of those Toccatas (brilliant 'touch' pieces) and fugues which are the ever-sustaining daily bread of every able organist to-day. The hardest job to learn was that of writing fugues: Bach's marvellous mastery was not gained without many fumbles.

It was at this time (1704) that Bach composed his one piece of real pictorial ('programme') music—a jest describing the dangers that might beset his brother John Jacob, who was going off to join the King of Sweden's guards' band. But apart from those suggestive touches in the chorale preludes, Bach was not a maker of programme-music, as the term is applied strictly—to purely instrumental works, though moments in certain organ works make us think he may have had some scene in mind.

A Holiday and its Consequences

Now, after a couple of years' steady service, Bach thought he was entitled to a good holiday, and for it he made a big plan: he would have the best holiday of his life—go on a far greater pilgrimage than any he had yet made, and visit one of his heroes, the famous master Buxtehude, who, now getting on for seventy, had been the organist at Lübeck's church of St. Mary for nearly forty years. The journey was over two hundred miles, as the crow flies (Lübeck lies up near Germany's northern coast), and on the often bad, rambling roads of the time it must have been a good deal more. It seems that Bach planned it as a combined walking and musical tour, for walk it he did—both ways, with probably some lifts on the road. Lübeck fascinated him, and it appears that there was some chance of succeeding to Buxtehude's post; but it was a custom of the day that the incoming organist should take also the retiring man's daughter, and, though the matter is not very clear, it seems that the prospect did not tempt Bach.

But Lübeck and its other opportunities did, with the result that, instead of being back at his organ by November 1705, to take over again from the cousin he had left as deputy,

it was February 1706 when he tramped into Arnstadt! You
can imagine the solemnities exercised by his church authorities over this terrible breach of duty. They could not be
expected to know how much the visit had done for Bach
the composer: it had been the greatest eye- and heart-opener
of his life; they were naturally concerned about their church
music: not least because Bach had not proved himself a good
disciplinarian (what diverse qualities are needed in the perfect
organist—qualities technical, imaginative, and organisatory!),
and had taken too little interest in the choir; also (there were
several admonishings, at intervals of some months) he had
put organ variations into the hymns, and so worried the
congregation—the sort of transport that every organist has
felt some day or other, when stirred by the richness of a fine
hymn: I feel sympathy with Bach over that more than anything else. There was, too, some mention of his having
once or twice slipped out during the sermon to a little house
across the road. . . . But the sermons may have been *very*
dry, and organ playing, we know, is dry work too. Last
but, O my dear friends, surely not least, Bach had allowed
his girl cousin (whom he was to marry within a year) to
sing in the choir, from which, of course, women, the dangerous creatures, were barred.

The place was obviously not congenial—though I must
say I think the church authorities let Bach off pretty lightly
about those three months of stolen holiday. Yet has not
each of us at least once found the regular round of work
so much of a treadmill that we have been tempted to smash
our way out, and play truant, at any cost? And Bach must
now have been feeling his powers rising up, and have been
irked, when he wanted to be composing, at having to attend
to church duties, and school a pack of choirboys, without
having the inborn knack for that. By the summer of the
year following that in which he had so tardily returned from
Lübeck, he had explored one or two good openings (for
something of his mettle was by now known, if only locally),
and had decided to accept a post at Mühlhausen, where, though

he asked no larger salary, the standing was better.   He appears
to have got rather less, indeed, than before, but there was an
addition in "kind"—some corn and wood.   It is difficult
to see how he could live comfortably, but though he never
attained a high salary, he seems to have been contented with
his modest means.   Here, on 17th October, 1707, at the age
of rather less than twenty-three, he married the little cousin
who had so disturbed the good Arnstadt folk, a small legacy
from an uncle coming handily to help them to set up house.

In Princely Service

But Mühlhausen did not provide the ideal conditions for
Bach's musical life.   Hitherto he had been among convinced
Lutherans of the orthodox kind; but here there were those
reforming specialists, whom we know, as the Pietists—the
sort of particularly strait brethren, fearing artistry in religion,
which almost every sect seems to throw up.   They had started
about 1670, and their opposition to the sort of worship music
that was necessary to Bach's development made it impossible
for him to work happily among the clamours of orthodoxy
v. Pietism; so, within the year, after writing a few cantatas
that showed rising mastery, Bach, leaving yet another cousin
to carry on the Mühlhausen organistship (the Bachs were apparently inexhaustible), made a bold move for better pay and
fewer vexations: no less an adventure than the post of organist
and concert master (though not supreme master of music)
to 'His Royal and Serene Highness of Saxe-Weimar.'

Weimar was quite a metropolis, of some five thousand
people.   The move was, financially, the best he had yet
made, his income now being about double the Mühlhausen
figure; and in his nine years there, Dr. Terry tells us, it was
doubled again.   His master was one of the worthiest of the
German princes, devoted to religion and good works, as
he saw them.   Here Bach had a small choir of about a dozen
to look after, and a fine organ, for which he wrote some of
his best works.   Certain of these we hear fairly often by
radio—the lusty 'fugue à la gigue,' for instance, which shows

at work the lighter Southern influences, under which he
came more strongly at Weimar than before.

Here, too, he first became known as an outstanding organ-
player, and gave recitals in neighbouring cities. At one of
them his pedalling so took the fancy of a prince that he gave
the nimble organist a valuable ring. The great Prelude
and Fugue in D, one of the modern recitalist's war-horses,
comes from this period; so does the Toccata and Fugue in
D minor with which the Philadelphia Orchestra, in Stokow-
ski's arrangement, made gramophone history, and new
friends for J. S. B. We can imagine Bach's delight in performing such new bravura pieces to fresh audiences at princely
houses, or to his own Prince, on the castle organ with its
grand 32-foot pedal stop. This bravura period is a strong
one, at Weimar, though in the latter part of his residence
there his increasing knowledge of Italian sacred music, of
which in his earlier years he can have met very little, brought
to his style a refinement and greater inwardness, such as we
find in the Fantasia and Fugue in C minor (the one that Elgar
orchestrated: it is recorded), and the great Passacaglia and
Fugue in C minor, which shows him in the great succession,
glorifying an old form. It is ill for an organist to have to
leave the great organ works of Bach without an overflow
of descriptive enthusiasm; yet this is essentially a book about
the man, not the music. For all organists, and many besides,
'Old Bach' is his name. The adjective bespeaks neither his
years nor his period: only their love.

Among other works of Bach's which are fairly often
broadcast in the 'Proms.' are his arrangements of some
violin concertos by the Italian Vivaldi, which he was writing
about this time—further evidence of the Southern influences
under which he came during this, his second period of experience. He thought nothing of arranging a concerto originally
written for four violins and orchestra, for four pianos and
orchestra, the weaving of the additional strands being, as
we might popularly put it, 'pie for him,' though a lasting
marvel to us.

A Win, Hands Down

The court orchestra, in which Bach played, had about twenty players, and here again his experience of music would be enlarged, not least because orchestras were only then beginning to stand on their own feet, with clearly formulated proportions of the various instruments. He was made 'Konzertmeister' in 1714, having to compose a monthly cantata, and to be on hand with new celebratory pieces for birthdays and weddings, fit music for funerals, and so forth. But he did not attain his ambition to become the real chief of all the music, the 'Kapellmeister,' and when this post fell vacant in 1716, and the Duke passed him over, Bach felt that he must seek a wider field. He was feeling, perhaps, a little elevated by the fact that a few months before he had agreed to a grand contest of performing-musicianship with one Marchand, the organist of Louis XV; but when Bach arrived for the event, Marchand, who had agreed to the contest, had thrown up the sponge by leaving the city. If that pleased Bach, there was little else to satisfy him at Weimar, and, a Kapellmeistership being offered him by the Prince of Anhalt-Cöthen, he went there at the end of 1717. He had not got away from Weimar without a fuss, for the Duke was apparently a rather cold-natured man, well aware of his rights, and of his dependents' dependency; and Bach had a temper. When he wanted to get away quickly, the ruler refused, and we get a hint of feudal powers in the record which tells us that Bach was arrested on 6th November 'in the justice's room on account of his obstinately insisting upon his resignation being accepted at once, and was finally set free on 2nd December and notified that he had been ungraciously allowed to resign.' Bach, we find, had had to attend on his master in livery: musicians in those days were only middle-class servants. Even a musician like Bach or Haydn (who also served princes) was only counted as one among a number of dependent, poorly paid vassals, who might be treated with coldness or with friendliness, according

to the nature of his prince. No wonder the democratic mind rebels when the beauties of feudalism are expounded!

At the Court of Cöthen

Bach was now thirty-two, a man with a wide reputation and three children living (a daughter and two sons: twins, born in 1713, only lived a few hours); with an insufficient income, no prospect of advancement at Weimar, and immediate need to get work. Small wonder that he took a post which was not quite the sort of thing he needed. The Cöthen court provided him with an opening for fresh experience, but he had to put aside his older form of productivity, for while Weimar had turned his activities largely into the fields so far most familiar—those of his first love, the organ, and the church cantata, Cöthen opened up his mind towards chamber music, and here we find him writing the first book of the immortal 'Forty Eight'—those preludes and fugues for the piano (harpsichord or clavichord, as it was then) which have been well described as 'the pianist's Old Testament': his New Testament being Beethoven's thirty-two sonatas. We find also those keyboard suites, of which the 'French' suites have been mentioned as a good introduction to his writings for the keyboard; together with music for the violin and violoncello; and the works that are perhaps best known of all to lay listeners—the Brandenburg Concertos for orchestra.

So Bach enters, during 1717 to 1723, on a new period of productivity, with as his master a younger, more amiable ruler, himself skilled with voice and violoncello, but in a court whose musical resources were rather small. However, the diversity of experience, and the change from the cares of organ and choir, with the requirements of cantata composing, went to build up in Bach the grand wholeness that we know. It seems, as we now see it, that his big change, even though it was not made in the happiest circumstances, was needed to give him the impetus for another side of

composition, one which was necessary not only to his development, but to that of the art of composition; for the instrumental side of that (apart from organ music) had, in Northern climes, lagged behind the choral. New strength was needed to bring on the art of chamber music. The Italians, with men like Corelli and Vivaldi, had done wonders for the violin, which had for years contested with the old viol family and, in the hands of makers like Amati, Gasparo da Salo, and Stradivari, had become in the seventeenth century an instrument of the most amazing possibilities. Bach's was not the nature to exploit those possibilities. Every man to his job; and Bach's chief world of interest lay in the church, among worship music; secondarily, in keyboard music, with its strong organ interest, again derived from the church; but yet his inventive mind enjoyed exploring the world of the orchestra, as far as it was then established, with its foundations of strings, and its sharp-toned oboes and bassoons as wood-wind, with the trumpets and horns to balance them in the brass, the drums bringing up the rear. His invention did not, however, lie in the direction of seeking the extension of this orchestral kingdom; rather, accepting it (as also did Handel), he sought interesting combinations within it, as we note in those six Brandenburg Concertos, which have such varying solo-groups set over against the main body of the band.

It is strange to think that so little of his music was printed in his lifetime, and that some of this was due to his own exertions with the engraving tool. Scarcely any of the so numerous cantatas appeared in print until he was dead. Indeed, we have to remember all along that his fame was very limited. As Sir Donald Tovey puts it: 'To the music-lovers of 1740 the annihilation of Bach and Handel would have meant the disappearance of Bononcini's successful rival and of an obscure scholar locally famous in Leipzig.'

Cantatas, however, were not lacking at Cöthen, for Bach enjoyed writing a few secular ones for high occasions, such as his ruler's birthday, or some distinguished person's wedding.

It seemed as if the Cöthen years might stretch out quietly, very far ahead. From one of those short tours with the prince which were so pleasant, Bach came back to find that his wife had died after a very short illness, and been buried before he could be informed and return. Their life together had been happy, in spite of his ups and downs. She, like his second wife, must have been a wonderful manager to rear four children (out of the seven she bore) on an income so small as his. Besides the twins mentioned above, who lived for so short a time, there had been one other infant, born in 1718, who had survived only a year. The eldest of the four living was only about twelve; of the other three, Wilhelm Friedemann and Carl Philipp Emmanuel were to become famous musicians and survive their father.

Anna Magdalena's Devotion and Reward

It was in 1721 that he took his second wife, the twenty-year-old daughter of a town musician, the Anna Magdalena who was to bear him thirteen children in the intervals of managing the house and the other four, of being taught music by her husband, and copying out his works, or setting the children at it. She was, alas, to die in something like poverty, living on a little town charity until 1760, ten years after her husband's death. Surely that speaks but poorly for her sons!

Before Bach's second marriage, as we have noted, he had put in a splendid period of composition at Cöthen, and during his six years there he enjoyed many fine and formative experiences. He visited again one of his old heroes, Reinken, who was nearly a centenarian, and who came out to hear his disciple give a performance, including an example of an art which is rare enough to-day—that of extemporisation: inventing music, in good form, upon a given theme. Reinken is said to have given his benediction to the exhibition in the words 'I thought that this art was dead, but I see that it still lives, in you.'

There was at this time, 1720, a chance of a church post

at Hamburg, where Reinken lived, but though Bach had strong supporters, the post was disposed of more on what we should call political-honours grounds than on those of musical powers, and Bach remained at Cöthen, perhaps a happy result, in that he was thus led to continue the production of chamber and orchestral music. We have to remember that Bach had many rivals, and probably only a minority of people would have voted him supreme in his day. Some of the rivals were preferred above him. Who has heard of Telemann? Yet he was by many esteemed above Bach, whose work, a generation after his death, was very little remembered.

To this 1720 period belongs the set of six sonatas for solo violin; and we may judge what can happen to the work of a master when we hear that nearly a century later, at the time when Mendelssohn was re-discovering Bach, the manuscript of these sonatas (Anna Magdalena wrote them out) was found 'among a pile of old papers in Petersburg, destined for the butter-shop.' Bach himself, we remember, was a fiddler, who spent some time in orchestras.

There are also from this period some sonatas for violin with keyboard, works in which we find that type of expression that the German word *innig*—deeply-felt, inward—so well describes. He wrote, too, for his nine-year old son Wilhelm Friedemann, a series of pieces which we know as the 'Clavier-Büchlein'—(Little Book for the Keyboard). In them he showed how to finger the music, in ways which helped greatly to develop the general technique of the keyboard. It is curious that in its early days the three middle fingers had nearly all the work, the little finger being less frequently used than the others, and the thumb rarest of all—because it was the shortest. Nowadays we bend the four fingers until all the tips, including the thumb's, lie in almost a straight line. So all are handy. This seems so obvious that we may wonder why it was not thought of in the beginning. The touch of the early keyboard instruments with strings (not of the organ) was so light that great facility was possible, even with a limited use of the two outer fingers; and since the tone could not be well sustained, there was no need to worry about 'joining the fingers'; one just rattled away, and the speed, with ornamentation, helped to give some illusion of continuity; but real sustaining power, as well as varied tone colour by finger pressure, was impossible, and so people reconciled themselves to such good qualities as the keyboard instruments offered. After all, 'you don't miss what you've never had.' Bach was one of the men (the French composer Couperin, whose music he had first heard at Celle, was another) who were planning a better system of fingering, with free use of the thumb—making it work under the other fingers, and perform as a full member of the tribe, instead of an apparently short-legged, crippled one.

The Scheme Behind the '48'

Bach the innovator appears again, in 1722, in the way perhaps best known to all of us, in his great collection of forty-eight preludes and fugues in all the keys, entitled in the original 'Das Wohltemperirte Clavier'—(The Well-Tempered Keyboard). Why 'well tempered'? Well, the old method of tempering (tuning) the keyboard was based on a system which (to put it briefly and as untechnically as possible) left some keys well in tune and some out of tune. Bach advocated little adjustments so that music in *every* key would be equally pleasant, even if the tuning were not mathematically exact. Such tuning is, of course, a commonplace to-day, but it was by no means so in Bach's time, or even for a good while afterwards. He had already, in improvising at the organ, illustrated his meaning by making swift moves from key to key, often so subtly moving to a distant key that the particular nature of the transition was not remarked, and a listener would be surprised suddenly to find himself in a key much further from that of the start than he had imagined. The sterling qualities of the '48' (only the first book appeared in 1722, containing twenty-four—one in each of the keys:

he produced the other volume in 1744) caused people to
want to play them. If they did, argued Bach, they would
have to have their instruments tuned in the way he wanted.
So he did two good works at once. The musician is again
tempted to dwell on the variety of mood and feeling in these
works. Not only is there a great diversity of styles in the
fugues (which, far from being a strict form, as some think,
is really the freest: a style, rather than a form, indeed), but
the preludes offer a surprising range of short impressions—
endless delight, in even greater freedom of form and fancy.
The idea that fugues are dull probably exists. A few days
spent with the '48' by anyone with ears to hear would
dispel it.

In the '48' there are many kinds of thought and feeling.
Only sentimentality is absent. That great church musician
who worked sturdily for a Bach revival, Samuel Wesley,
called the E major fugue in Book II of the '48' 'The Saints in
Glory.' Its lovely serenity makes the name very fitting, to
my ears, and I like to use it. This is one of the instances in
which it seems no hindrance, but a help, to allow a mental
picture, or suggestion of mood, to colour a piece that has no
title. Who can tell what pictures Bach may have had in
mind when writing his works? You will find all manner
of types side by side in the '48'—ripe dignity, for example,
in No. 4 of Book I, and pomp and circumstance of another
kind in No. 5; while next to the 'Saints' in Book II is a piece
of cheerful, marching mundanity. Well are the '48' called
a 'Testament,' for they testify not only to Bach's faith in a
tuning system now commonplace, although then deemed
by some a dangerous novelty, but also to his faith in the power
of woven music to move and delight us.

The Lordly Concerto Collector

The often heard Brandenburg Concertos belong to the
mid-Cöthen period. Bach, in the course of his small
journeys and his visits to other centres, had come across

yet another of the numerous music-loving princes, the Mark-graf of Brandenburg, who in modern terms would be described as a 'concerto-fan,' he having played the happy part of patron to a number of composers whom he had invited to write works for him. Bach's reply to the invitation was a hearty one: he wrote six concertos, dedicating them to the prince with an address in French, very humble, as became a mere musician to his patron: mentioning his 'small talent,' the patron's 'fine and delicate taste,' by the severity of which, he prayed, their imperfections might not be judged, but begging him to take into his benign consideration the profound respect of the composer, to continue his good graces towards him, and 'to be persuaded that I have nothing so much at heart as the wish to be employed in occasions more worthy of You and of Your service—I who am with un-paralleled zeal, Monseigneur, Your Royal Highness's most humble and very obedient servant, Jean Sebastien Bach.'

Typical of the feudal spirit, but not quite typical of the best spirit of J. S. B. Probably he used the extremely flatter-ing and self-abasing terms more as an expected formula than with his heart's belief in the prince's superior judgment and his own imperfections. But real humbleness about his gifts was a notable attribute of Bach. For the rest, he had to conform to the age in which he found himself. He was never rich, and in the eighteenth century the level of inde-pendence was high, and the number of those who could afford to be independent very few. I wish we could be sure that the Markgraf paid well—even the compliments deserved that; but we have no information as to how he valued the concertos. We do know, however, how posterity valued them: at about fivepence apiece. This was when an inventory of the Markgraf's collection was made, after his death; and Bach's music was not even given under his name: it was lumped with a pile of other concertos. Though we may reckon the value of money as a good deal greater in 1734, and call fivepence half a crown or even, to be really generous, three shillings, that does not seem quite the right figure for a Brandenburg Concerto that has given delight to millions.

To about this same time the four orchestral suites belong. These lay dormant for several generations after Bach's death, and not until 1853, long after Mendelssohn had laboured to make Bach known again, were they published.

Not long after his marriage Bach made a little set of pieces to teach his wife to play the harpsichord. 'Anna Magdalena's Clavier Book' has been used for many students' edification since that time when, we like to think, Anna, having cleared a short spell from housework and children, sat down at the keyboard, and Johann Sebastian sat beside her and affectionately guided her fingers.

Back to His First Love

Soon after this Bach seems to have felt again the pull of church work, which his Cöthen period had denied him. His prince, too, appeared to think more of a new wife that he had taken, than of music—perhaps she did not think a great deal of music at all: Bach thought so. He had the chance to go to Leipzig, the great city of 30,000 people, to the famous St. Thomas's church. Though it seemed rather a come-down to exchange the high title of Kapellmeister for that of Cantor, with the possibilities of being hampered by parson and committee, the certainty of pretty strict rules (such as that he must not leave the city without permission from the mayor), and with choirboys on his hands again, yet there would be better education for his children, and he could still keep some visiting work at Cöthen and elsewhere. After some doubt he entered for the post, was tested, and appointed to succeed the distinguished Kuhnau whom we now remember chiefly for some charming examples of early programme music, his 'Bible Sonatas.'

So in May 1723 he was settled in the post that he was to hold until his death; and we find beginning his greatest period of sacred composition. As Cantor he had not to play the organ, but to train the boys for their work in two churches (teaching Latin as well as music—singing and playing), to direct the choirs, which sang with an orchestra, and to please not only the church authorities but also the Town Council, who governed the 'Thomasschule,' and the University people, for it was also his duty to train its Musical Society. The pleasing involved, unfortunately, something more difficult than the able performance of professional duties, for there was an old controversy about who should be music master of the university chapel. Controversies of one kind or another were easily found in Leipzig musical circles, and even the School did not continue to provide the best musical material for Bach's ministrations; some of it was not very good when he went there, and there was trouble in 1729, when new scholars fell to be elected, and Bach's choice was not entirely followed by his Council masters. Of some of the town musicians who played in his orchestra he said next year: 'Discretion prevents me from revealing anything near the truth about their quality . . .; they are partly past their work. . . .'

His income is given by Parry as about £70 a year (worth, to-day, nearly £500), much of it dependent on special fees, for weddings, funerals, part of the students' carol-singing money, and so forth. When the year was particularly mild, and fewer people died, Bach suffered. He suffered, too, from one or two unsympathetic Rectors of the School, though there was a happy spell from 1730 to 1734, under Gesner, an appreciator from Weimar days. The next Rector was young and masterful. Music was to be put in its place, and the Cantor in his: thus, new conflicts of authority. The Council, to whom Bach appealed, hummed and hawed, and managed to avoid deciding. Bach, afraid of nobody, took the matter to the king (he had gone as high as that once before; and he was now a Court Composer). His Majesty seems to have been sympathetic, and to have decided for Bach; but that, we can understand, would cause the Rector, in his chagrin, not to lose any opportunity of hindering Bach elsewhere.   Bach had come at a weak period in the School's history; and he was not the man joyfully to put up with hindrances to his work.   He never had a sufficient force to supply his several churches : it ran to only about fifteen or twenty for each—and this for the biggest works, in double choruses.   Then, the musicians for the church orchestras were still less numerous and efficient, and sometimes singers had to be got, somehow, to play, with a consequent depletion of the small singing force.   Probably the Council meant well, on the whole—better than the Rector; but Bach, in the full force of his greatest creative period, must have been wearied with his insufficient performers, with having to teach, and with recurring controversies, in which his temperament did not allow him to see any prerogative challenged without fighting for it.   He may have neglected some of his duties; but if only the authorities could have measured aright the stature of the genius who had come among them, and have freed him for composition !   No strong-minded, upright man could have held Bach's Leipzig posts without making enemies.   When to all else is added the power of genius, that must always know its own superfine quality : and when he had to bear one domestic bereavement after another, to the number of seven children out of the thirteen born at Leipzig—with, towards the end, the loss of his eyesight, we can well understand what a spirit must be in such a man, if he is to produce the choicest fruits of his genius under these conditions.

Concertos at Home

The children that remained were, almost all of them, a great joy to him.   Several became distinguished composers, and one, Carl Philipp Emmanuel, was a strong link between Bach and Haydn, because of the work he did in developing the form of the sonata.   Wilhelm Friedemann, the eldest son, was a fine keyboard player and improviser, and had something of his father's wide capacity in composition.

Johann Christoph Friedrich, Anna Magdalena's eldest son, became a court composer, and Johann Christian, Anna's youngest son, came to London (he is hence called the 'London Bach') and lived the last twenty years of his short life (1735–1782) among us. One son only, Bernhard, was a bit of a black sheep: chiefly laziness and debt. But though several of the surviving children did well, there might have been a far larger tribe of able Bachs, had it not been for the very bad infant death-rate in that century. Only one of the seven children of Anna Magdalena that died at Leipzig lived to be more than three years old; and at Bach's death his surviving children numbered nine, out of the twenty that his two wives bore him. Dr. Sanford Terry points out that when Bach could afford a better house, fewer of his children died. The M.O.H. was sadly lacking in those days. But even when only a small muster of the family was present, they could have grand music-makings together. In a letter to a friend in 1730, Bach says of his brood: 'They are all born musicians, and I can assure you that I can already hold a concert, both vocal and instrumental, in my own family; my wife sings a very clear soprano and my eldest daughter joins in bravely.' It would have been a very queer member of that family, one surmises, that did *not* join in! One of the family's diversions was singing 'quodlibets.' These 'what-you-wills' were simply stringings together of various melodies at one time, the skill of the singers shaping the whole into something like harmony. It would be a bewildering practice for us to-day, but it was popular well before Bach's time.

Turn we now to those great works of Bach's long final period—the greatest of the cantatas, the motets (extended anthems), the 'Passions,' the 'Mass,' supreme among such works. The music of the Lutheran Church was his life's consuming fire, that burned most richly at Leipzig. Her dogmatic doctrine, too, he revered. His faith was unshakable. A great deal of that music was written in the Leipzig period—the great bulk of nearly three hundred

B

cantatas, for instance, being the product of the need for week-by-week choral works. If he did not seek to keep up the supply of new ones for the whole of that time, he did produce, with apparent ease, an average of a cantata every month for over twenty years, most of them works of some extent, with choruses large or small, several arias, instrumental interludes, and hymn settings (chorales), Bach's harmonisations of which are every student's standard, and sometimes his despair. Here, as in the preludes on the tunes, Bach pointed the meaning of the words in poignant harmonies.

Bach the Ready Writer

Character shows in handwriting. A Munich firm, Drei Masken Verlag, has reproduced in faithful facsimile complete works by the great composers. The Bach example is a cantata, fascinating in its actuality. Bach begins neatly enough, but soon there are urgent corrections. Sometimes he crosses out; at others he just blotches the first thought with his thumb, and writes the better one above the smear. His quill loses its point; blots appear. I wonder if 'language' was heard also? As a sympathetic beholder of this human document remarked, the writing suggests the composer's sitting down late in the week to produce a cantata for Sunday. The note-shaping is boldly characteristic, if not as handsome as Mendelssohn's or Wagner's (the latter's was surely the most beautiful of all great composers'). Here is a man who makes up his mind in a trice: perhaps it is not too much to deduce, a man who has a temper! We ought to put a calligraphic expert on to these admirable reproductions of the Drei Masken Verlag.

There are four settings of the Passion story, very interesting for the lover of Bach to compare. There are in them, too, arias and choruses, some of them very dramatic and some reflective. The best known of these, one that happily is to be heard from a good many choirs at Easter, is 'The St.

Matthew Passion' (1729), and the next best known that which sets the story according to St. John (1723). 'The Christmas Oratorio' (1733-4) has always been overshadowed here, in popular knowledge and esteem, by Handel's 'Messiah,' naturally enough, since Handel himself established the popularity of his work in this country, and since his music is, as has been remarked, easier at first to take in than Bach's, being more objective, and not so fully woven. Bach's work is much longer, also, as it was written in six parts, each for use on a separate day. Hence it has not the conciseness and the easily traceable dramatic sequences of Handel's work. But it has been more frequently performed of late years, and there would perhaps be no harm if, in order to make it still more widely known in churches, part of it were given instead of 'The Messiah,' once in a way, until people became accustomed to its special beauties, which might then be looked forward to as are the old favourites in Handel.

There is also an Easter oratorio, which Bach twice revised (as he did the St. John passion music); one of the surest signs of greatness is this willingness to prune and the ability to perfect a work thereby. A third oratorio, so called, is of smaller dimensions—a cantata for Ascensiontide (1735-6). Besides six extended anthems (motets), there are several Masses, the greatest being the one in B minor, often described briefly as 'the Bach Mass' or 'the B min or.' The word 'mass' does not, of course, carry the same significance in Lutheran worship as in the older faith. It was a shortened form. The B minor Mass, that by the triumph of Bach's skill appears so unified, was made up of several parts, composed at different times. It began as the ordinary short Lutheran Mass—Kyrie and Gloria—which Bach, in the midst of his struggles with the School authorities in 1733, sent to the ruler of Saxony, with one of the very humble petitions of which we have already seen a sample, praying that the king would grant him an appointment as Court Composer. This he thought would give him a firmer standing with his

own people.   His Majesty was for some time too busy with
wars to attend, but the petition, as we have seen, was granted
in 1736.   For some of the remaining movements of this far
greater-scaled Mass he drew upon his cantatas (he was accustomed to use a piece in more than one place, if he found
it convenient: but he did not go to Handel's length in
borrowing, from his own works or those of other composers).   About 1738 the complete Mass in B minor was
ready; and though it is happily now known to a great many
good choirs, and has been heard at least once by millions of
people, it might be well to reckon 1938 as its bi-centenary
year, and ensure then the greatest possible dissemination of
this marvellous work, the like of which is to be found in the
music of no other composer: the highest point of sublimity,
the greatest depth of inspiration, musicians agree, that the
world has ever known in the music of religion.

A Kingly Command

With it we may well take leave of Bach, looking back to
note one of his last great pleasures, when, in 1747, he yielded
to the many requests of Frederick the Great, in whose service
his son Carl Philipp Emmanuel was, and journeyed to
Potsdam.   This was the most gratifying of the numerous
small trips that Bach made in his latter years.   He was in
request to advise about organs, and to open new ones with
recitals.   His interest in the keyboard and in music for it
came up strongly again, and there was less need to compose
new cantatas.

The Potsdam visit was paid just as Frederick was about
to begin some chamber-music making (he played the flute).
When Frederick was told, he exclaimed with delight, 'Gentlemen, old Bach has arrived!' and commanded the master
to come at once, before he had time to change his clothes.
Then Bach must try all the king's pianos (the 'forte-pianos,'
which Silbermann had supplied, he being the first German
to make them), improvising here and there on a theme

suggested by the royal amateur, and building up a six-part fugue on a theme of his own. The next day the king took him to try the Potsdam organs; and when Bach got home he worked out the king's theme, and, mindful of his being a flautist, included in his work a trio for flute, violin and keyboard. This 'Musical Offering' he sent to the king.

Bach had all his life been an assiduous copyist of his own and other people's music, often, we may guess, in an indifferent light. His eyes began to fail towards the end, and in spite of an operation by a famous surgeon (who also operated upon Handel), nothing could be done. A pathetic fact is that a few days before he died his sight came back, but paralysis brought the end on July 28th, 1750. He was buried first in St. John's churchyard, without (it seems strange) any memorial; and only in 1894 was his coffin discovered and reinterred in the church.

BIBLIOGRAPHY

FORKEL, JOHANN NIKOLAUS: *Johann Sebastian Bach; his Life, Art and Work.* Translated by C. S. TERRY. 21s. (Constable, 1920.)

MEYNELL, ESTHER: *Bach.* 2s. (Duckworth, 'Great Lives' Series, 1933.)

MEYNELL, ESTHER: *The Little Chronicle of Anna Magdalena Bach.* 3s. 6d. (Chapman & Hall, 1934.)

PARRY, C. H. H.: *Bach, the Story of the Development of a Great Personality.* 6s. (Putnam, 1934.)

SCHWEITZER, ALBERT: *J. S. Bach.* Translated by ERNEST NEWMAN. 2 vols. Second edition. 30s. (Black, 1935.)

SPITTA, PHILIPP: *Johann Sebastian Bach.* Translated by CLARA BELL and J. A. FULLER MAITLAND. 3 vols. 42s. (Novello, 1898.)

TERRY, C. SANFORD: *Bach; a Biography.* 21s. (Oxford University Press, 1928.)

TERRY, C. SANFORD: *Bach; the Historical Approach.* 7s. 6d. (Oxford University Press, 1930.)

WILLIAMS, ABDY: *Bach.* Revised by ERIC BLOM. 4s. 6d. (Dent, 1933.)

WILLIAM BYRD

BORN 1543   DIED 4 July 1623

By Richard Runciman Terry

Music and the Man

How did it come to pass that the nobility and gentry of England—distinguished by exceptional talent in the art of music in Tudor times—had by the eighteenth century become philistines of the deepest dye? That, alas, is a question to which history furnishes no reasonable answer.

How did it come to pass that the Universities of Oxford and Cambridge—seats of learning; homes of culture; in whose curricula music once took its honoured place among the liberal arts—had by the eighteenth century become so criminally careless in the matter of musical documents that, to-day, among the priceless MSS. committed to their custody we find too many of them with part-books missing, mutilated, or otherwise incomplete? No answer.

How did it come to pass that an England, once in the forefront of European musical culture, had by the eighteenth century accepted it as an axiom that the pursuit of music was 'no occupation for scholars and gentlemen'? Again no answer.

All these facts, however, taken together, do furnish some sort of a clue to the reason why we now possess such scanty information concerning our Tudor composers, compared with their Continental contemporaries. But explanations need not detain us here. They cannot restore a knowledge that once was, and now is not.

Certain recorded incidents in Byrd's career do furnish some small amount of biographical material, but it is safe to say that, taken by and large, the greatest names in Tudor music rarely yield up more biographical matter than would cover Balfour's historic 'half sheet of notepaper.' So if we seek to know what manner of men they were, we must fall back on their music and draw from it what deductions we can. This is easier to do with Byrd than with his contemporaries. His output was greater, his range wider; his excursions into the unknown were more daring. His architecture was more spacious; his line of march is more clearly defined, step following step in logical and well-ordered progression. As we follow him, his artistic purpose does take shape before us. More than that; since he was primarily a vocal composer, his choice of verbal texts also gives us some insight into his prevailing temper of mind and trend of thought, into his emotional reactions and his æsthetic outlook.

For the general reader, purely musical analysis is of little help to the understanding of a composer; nor is it of much use to the musical one who has not the score before him (or a gramophone handy), unless he has studied it beforehand. But the most casual reader cannot fail to catch something of a composer's spirit if he is referred to the printed verbal texts that inspire the music. A man's literary bent is a strong indication of his personality and Byrd reveals himself very fully in this respect. We see him as the typical cultured Englishman of the period, 'when life was lived in many-gabled houses and the Thames flowed unpolluted' to the sea and all things were fair and clean'; when the pleasant land was tended and tilled and the treacherous sea defied and conquered; when high adventure attended Englishmen overseas and a wide culture filled their lives at home; and, behind all, the presence of a religious duel to the death, when the nation is to be seen—in typically English fashion—adapting its daily life to the inevitable with the humoursome absence of philosophy that has served it so well in every great crisis. We see Byrd moving through those stirring times with the same outward serenity, but with the inward consciousness (as will appear later) of the bigness of events and the vastness of the

issues at stake.   Such clear perspective is, in the main, denied
to the Englishman who lives through troubled times (as witness the last war).   It is given only to the man of clear vision
and contemplative mind to shape his interior life and rule
his outward action in the light of what is passing around him.
He realises the true meaning of all that is happening.   Circumstances may occupy his *thought*; they do not rule his *life*;
he remains captain of his soul.

To outward appearance Byrd was the product of his time,
summing up in his person all that the sixteenth century had
to say in music, and by his genius adding to all that had been
said, in his daring excursions down untrodden paths and
across uncharted seas.   Studied more closely, his music
reveals him as a personality of absorbing human interest.
Before consideration of the music in detail it is well to give
the scanty records of his social and professional career.

From Lincolnshire to Middlesex

Byrd was born in Lincolnshire in 1543.   The date is established by the statement in his Will (in 1622) that he was then
in his eightieth year.   The place is uncertain; no record
exists, and the claim for Epworth rests on rather flimsy
evidence.   Equally untenable is Byrd's supposed descent
from one Henry Byrd, a former Mayor of Newcastle, who
died at Lincoln in 1512.   Nothing is known with certainty
about the first twenty years of his life, but Anthony Wood's
statement that Byrd was 'bred up to musick under Thomas
Tallis' would indicate that some of his early life was spent in
London, Tallis being then at the Chapel Royal.   In February
1563 he was appointed organist of Lincoln Cathedral.   In
1568 he married Juliana (? Ellen) Birley who bore him six
(some say five) children.   When Robert Parsons, a Gentleman of the Chapel Royal, was drowned in the Trent in 1569,
Byrd was sworn in as his successor, but he must have continued for some time to perform his duties at Lincoln as well,
for the record exists of his daughter Elizabeth's baptism there

(in January 1572). In December of the same year his connection with Lincoln ceased on the appointment of Thomas
Butler as his successor (on Byrd's own nomination). At the
Chapel Royal he shared the duties of organist with his old
master, Tallis. Of his residence in London, where he
appears to have had chambers in the house of the Earl of
Worcester, records are wanting, but in 1578 we hear of his
having a house at Harlington, a Middlesex village about
11 miles from London; he lived there for some fourteen or
fifteen years, performing the while such duties as his Chapel
Royal post required. The reasons for this life in a little
village, so far removed from the scene of his professional
work (in those days of bad roads 11 miles was a formidable
journey) are not so puzzling as might appear at first sight, if
we remember that, first, Byrd was a Catholic and, secondly,
London was the headquarters of the reforming party and the
rendezvous of Protestant refugees from the Continent. It
therefore seems probable that Byrd, on the principle of 'out
of sight, out of mind,' deemed it prudent to show himself
as little as possible in a city where feeling ran high and the
agent provocateur was unpleasantly active.

This supposition is not unreasonable, as he did not go
unmolested even at Harlington. As early as 1577 his wife
appears on the Bishop's list of 'Popish recusants' and, together
with a household servant, he and his wife appear as 'Popish
recusants' in the Session Rolls of Middlesex each year from
1581 to 1586. That Byrd escaped the extremest penalty of
the law is doubtless accounted for by the fact of his having
powerful friends and also because Elizabeth had her full
share of the Tudor love of music and was not the one to allow
interference with her domestic musicians, so long as they lay
low and kept outside the clutches of the law. If they failed
to do so she, of course, had no alternative but to allow the
law to take its course. Her attitude comes out amusingly
in the matter of one Bolt or Bold of the Chapel Royal.
Bold (living up to his name, let us say) had been indiscreet
in his talk and found it necessary to fly the country to escape

arrest. Elizabeth betrayed no anger at his 'popish' escapade but 'sent for her Master of Musicke,' rated *him* soundly for not looking better after a musician whose loss she could ill afford, and ended the interview by flinging her slipper at his head.

In spite of protection in high quarters, there is no doubt that Byrd was a marked man during this period. His name appears in a State Paper of 1583, concerning 'an inventory of the books and other Popish relics' found in the house of a Mr. Hampden of 'Stocke in the county of Bucks.' It is there set forth that a song-book had been sent to one recusant and a letter to another by 'one Mr. Byrd of the Queen's Majesty's Chapel.' The Domestic State Papers of Elizabeth mention Byrd's name in connection with a list of places 'where certain recusants remain in and about London' and also in another, giving the names of 'such as are relievers of papists and conveyors of money and other things unto them beyonde the Seas.'

Music at Harlington

Yet in spite of these troubles, which merit no softer name than persecution, this period at Harlington was one prolific in musical composition. 1575 saw the publication of a volume of Latin 'Cantiones,' the joint work of himself (with 18 Motets) and Thomas Tallis (with 16). In 1589 appeared his own first volume of 'Cantiones' for five voices. Another set for five or six voices appeared in 1591. Of secular music, his 'Psalms, Sonnets and Songs' appeared in 1588, the 'Songs of Sundry Natures' in 1589. ('Psalms, Songs and Sonnets' did not appear until 1611.)

The volume of 'Cantiones' issued by Tallis and Byrd in 1575 was the first to be printed under a licence, granted in that year by Queen Elizabeth, giving 'unto our well-beloved servaunts Thomas Tallis and William Birde Gentl. of our Chapell' a monopoly of all music-printing and ruling of music paper for a period of twenty-one years. The licence also forbade the importation into England of 'any songe or songes made and printed in any forren countrie, to sell or put to sale, uppon paine of our high displeasure.' Here was surely a lucrative privilege; on the strength of it they sublet part of it to others. Whether these others were too 'slim' as business men for the two composers will never be known, but we do know that in less than two years they were petitioning the Queen for an annuity of some sort (they were deliciously vague as to its nature), as the monopoly had proved a failure and they were 200 marks out of pocket. They got their annuity and retained the monopoly as well. After Tallis died in 1585, Byrd became sole proprietor. He eventually made Thomas East his assignee and East continued to print Byrd's music even after the lease expired in 1596.

After the publication (under Elizabeth's patent) of the Tallis-Byrd 'Cantiones' there is a gap of thirteen years in Byrd's otherwise prolific period at Harlington. The silence was broken by the inclusion of two settings of Ariosto's 'La Verginella' in a collection of madrigals entitled 'Musica Transalpina' issued by Nicholas Yonge, an enthusiastic musical amateur. As the greatest composers in Europe were laid under contribution—Palestrina, Marenzio, di Lasso, Vecchi, Nanini and others—the presence of Byrd's name in such high company is a marked tribute to his prestige already at that time.

Essex and some Litigation

We next hear of him at Stondon Place in Essex—a farm of 200 acres, near Ongar, which he obtained by purchase about 1593. Here he seems to have become something of a country gentleman (he did not, however, relinquish his Chapel Royal post), as he assumed a coat-of-arms which was officially recognised at the Herald's Visitation of Essex during the occupancy of the property by his grandson, Thomas Byrd.

The occupancy of Stondon Place gives us a lively picture

of William Byrd the citizen, as distinct from William Byrd the artist. Only after fifteen years of intermittent litigation was he able to establish his title to the estate, which he obtained under circumstances that were, to say the least, curious and involved. The property was originally part of the estates of William Shelley who, after having been committed to the Fleet Prison in 1580 and to the Tower in 1583 on the ground of complicity in a 'Popish plot' was finally attainted in 1586 and condemned to death. He too possibly had powerful friends, for the death-sentence was not carried out, though his estates were sequestrated. William and Laurence Hollingsworth had obtained a twenty-one years' lease of Stondon from Mr. Shelley and had divided the property between them, Laurence sub-letting his share to one Lolly. Laurence died, and William bought up the sole right to the lease from the Crown, but did not disturb Lolly. He next mortgaged his lease to one William Chambers, and in 1593 he and Chambers sold the farm outright to Byrd for £300. Lolly still remained in occupancy as tenant, and for two years paid his rent to Byrd. He then refused further payment, on the ground that Byrd had taken possession of 'certain houses and roomes' which he had held under the Hollings-worths. Byrd sued him and won his action in the Court of Chancery. Having gained his point, he was magnanimous enough not to eject Lolly and allowed him to remain until his lease ran out in 1597. To regularise the whole matter Byrd established his title to the property by securing a lease from the Crown for the lives of himself and his children Christopher, Elizabeth and Rachel. But any hopes he may have had of quiet possession were soon dashed. Shelley died in 1597 and his widow petitioned the Queen for the restoration of Stondon Place, on the ground that it was originally her property and not Shelley's, being part of her marriage jointure. It appears that Elizabeth was willing to allow Mrs. Shelley to receive the rents of the estate, but not to live on it. Byrd therefore remained at Stondon and Mrs. Shelley was ordered to allow him peaceful possession of the property. This state of affairs lasted until Elizabeth's death. On the accession of James I, Mrs. Shelley again pressed her claim with the result that, on payment of £10,000 to the Crown plus £1,000 compensation to Lord Effingham (who had already applied for a grant of the estates), she was granted possession of all her property and promptly gave Byrd notice to quit Stondon. As he had paid £300 for his rights and as he further claimed to have spent a considerable sum in improving the property he refused to move, put his case before the King and received James's support in a document that is unusual enough to bear quotation:

'Jan. 24th, 1604. The King to Mrs. Jane Shelley.

'We lately upon your suit delivered you your jointure lands, being our inheritance, which the late queen refused to do. But you use our said grant contrary to our meaning to the undoing of our servant, William Bird, Gentleman of our Chapel. He took leases of your farm and woods of Stondon Place, in the County of Essex, now parcel of your jointure, from the late queen for three of his children's lives, paid fines and bestowed great charges on the house and barns, paid his rent ever since the death of your husband, and deserved well of you. Yet notwithstanding you go about to thrust him out of his possessions to his present undoing having no other house, and to the great danger of his children's future estate. For staying of which your hard course, neither your own conscience, nor our benignity towards you, nor the decrees of our Exchequer Chamber yet in force, nor the letters of our Privy Council, nor any reasonable composition offered you by our said servant, move you. Being a woman of great living and no charge, and having many better houses than his, we marvel that in those lands which you so lately received from us, and which are our inheritance, you offer so hard measure to our servant. Whereupon we require you to permit him to enjoy the said farm and woods, and give no cause hereafter for complaint.'

Mrs. Shelley was a determined woman. She waited four years and then petitioned Robert Cecil, now become Earl of

Salisbury, for the restoration of Stondon, pleading that she was over three score years of age and now had no place near London save Stondon 'wherein to rest herself at this period of life.' She set forth the following grievances against Byrd:

'(1) That Bird being in quiet possession of Stondon place began a suit against your Sup^t in the Exchequer Chamber tenne yeares since, and the same pursued her sithence in his wief's & childrens names, praying thereby that the Court would order her to ratifie his lease, which he had from her late Matie for three lives.

'(2) Not prevailing herein, he thereupon stirred upp all the late Queen's patentees which held any part of her jointure lands, and did combyine himself with them to mainteyne severall suits against her for the same, which contynued about eight years, and procured her rents to be sequestered, and hath caused her to expend at least 1000^li in defence of her title.

'(3) Sir Thomas ffludd, Mr. Churchyard and the rest of the Queen's patentees upon notice of his highness letters patent granted upon your Sup^t for enjoying of her lands did surcease their suits and all submitted themselves, saving the said Bird and one Petiver, who being encouraged by the said Bird did a long tyme continue obstinate untill of late he likewise submitted himself. ffor which the said Bird did give him vile and bitter words for doing the same.

'(4) He hath likewise practised to disgrace her with divers her honorable friends and others of great quallite p^rsuading them that she was a woman of no good conscience and that she was about to put him out of his living without any just cause or title thereunto.

'(5) And being told by your Sup^ts Counsell in her presence that he had no right to the said living, hee both then and at other tymes before her said that yf he could not hould it by right, he would holde it by might, which course he hath pursued ever since.

'(6) The said Bird hath cutt downe great store of tymber Trees worth one hundred marks growing in the grounds belonging to the said place, hath felled all the underwoods worth 100^li and made therein greate spoile and greater would have made had not the ho^{ble} Court of Exchequer taken order to the contrary.

'(7) The lands in question are yearely worth 100£ for the which he hath onely paid 40 marks p an for syx yeares or thereabouts. But since the said letters patents, which beare date the ffyst day of September in the ffirst yeare of his highnes Raigne, he hath paid nothing at all; howbeit by the said Letters patents she was to receave the mean profytte thereof ever since the death of her husband who died about vii yeares since.

'(8) That for wante of this house your Sup^t was inforced in this last plague to remove from Towne to Towne, from whence being driven by reason of the plague there, she was at the last constrayned to lye at a tenants house of hers, neare Colchester far unfitting for her to her great disgrace and to the great hurt of your Supt, being unable in respect of her age to travaile upp and downe the country.

'All wch notwithstanding in her bounden duty to yor hono^r and with a reverence respect to yor Lo^{ps} motion; shee will be content to release all her charges, also the moyety of tharrerages aforesaid although with exceeding clamor he hath justly moved her to afford him no favour.'*

Cecil's endorsement of the document, with the rather curt conclusion, runs as follows:

'27 October 1608.

'This matter hath bene depending in Court and therefore lett her represent unto the Barons that which she hath there delivered unto me, who are better acquainted with the whole proceedings than I am, and will take some leysure to heare her complaint for I have none.

'R. Salisbury.'

Mrs. Shelley's suit went through the Courts and dragged on until her death in 1610, when Byrd cut the Gordian Knot by purchasing the estate outright from her son. The whole affair is curious. At first sight it does seem hard that Byrd,

* 7 James I, *Exchequer Decrees and Orders.*

a Catholic, should take possession of the confiscated estate of another Catholic, and the indomitable Mrs. Shelley is no doubt entitled to much sympathy. But on the other hand Byrd purchased his lease, not from Mrs. Shelley, but from the then legal holders of it, and he very naturally asked her where he 'came in' if he handed over to Mrs. Shelley, without compensation, what he had bought (for hard cash down) from someone else. It might also be urged that Byrd was not a rich man and the loss of his only property would be a serious matter. On the other hand, Mrs. Shelley's (aforesaid) payment of £11,000, a huge sum in those days, proclaimed her a wealthy woman to whom the loss of a small farm would not mean so much. And there can be little doubt that Byrd did the magnanimous thing in securing peace by re-purchasing what he had already paid for seventeen years previously.

Contemporary Witness

A musical examinee once described Bach as 'a numerous parent.' Byrd had the misfortune to be 'a numerous litigant' with varying success. His law cases may be tedious reading, but they do at least bring out points of his character into clear relief—his tenacity when fighting for what he deemed his rights; his magnanimity in the hour of victory; his resignation in the face of defeat. He is perhaps best described as a litigant devoid of the litigious spirit. Quarrelsome characters sometimes command respect but never affection. It was Byrd's lot to command affection to a degree almost unparalleled in musical history. The affection he inspired in his master Tallis is a matter of common knowledge; his pupil Morley dedicated to him his *Plaine and Easie Introduction to Practicall Musicke* 'to notifie unto youre selfe . . . the entire love and unfained affection which I bear unto you.' Elsewhere Morley speaks of him as 'never without reverence to be named of the musitians.' Other contemporary tributes to his genius as a musician and his character as a man would cover more pages than are here available, but they give us the picture of a grave and lovable character with that magnetic power of attraction that belongs only to strong men.

I have spoken of his wide culture and his sane outlook on life. For confirmation of this one has only to read through the texts, now available in book form, which he chose for his madrigals and songs, and also to note the fine literary sense that pervades the Prefaces to his published works, where he writes in both Latin and English with equal grace of style, shrewd wisdom and kindly humour. His character is perhaps best summed up in his Will—a clear-headed document, devoid of that fluidity of mind and flabbiness of thought with which the 'learned' commonly credit the musician. It was first published in full in *The Musician* of 2nd June, 1897, and is now available in Fellowes's *William Byrd*. Here is the preamble:

'In the name of the most glorious and undivided Trinitye Father sonne holy Goste three distinct persons and one eternall God Amen! I William Byrd of Stondon Place in the p^{ar}ish of Stondon in the Countye of Essex gentleman doe now in the 80th yeare of myne age but through ye goodness of God beeinge of good health and p^{er}fect memory make & ordayne this for my last will & Testament: First: I give & beequeth my soule to God Almyghtye my Creattor & redemer and preserver: humblye cravinge his grace and mercye for ye forgivenes of all my Synnes and offences: past p^{re}sent and to come. And y^t I may live and dye a true and p^{er}fect member of his holy Catholycke Church wthout wch I beeleve theire is noe Salvation for mee my body to bee honnestly buryed in that p^{ar}ish and place wheire it shall please God to take mee out of this lyve wch I humbly desire yf soe it shall please God maye bee in the parish of Stondon wheire my dwellynge is: And then to be buried neare unto the place where my wife lyest buryed. or else wher as God & the tyme shall p^{er}mytt & Suffer.'

This Will is dated 15th November, 1622. Byrd died in the following year, but not before he had given the world two immortal volumes of 'Gradualia.' The first appeared in 1605 and the second in 1607. A corrected edition of Vol. 1 was printed in 1610, which is fortunate, as all copies of the original imprint have disappeared. It is worth noting that between 1591 and 1605 we have another interval when nothing appears from Byrd's pen. True, he did—'in friendly contention' with Alfonso Ferrabosco—set a *canto fermo* 'in 40 severall waies.' This was published in 1603, but no copy now exists. The writer of the article on Byrd in Grove's *Dictionary* is probably right in accounting for the silence by the fact that Byrd was then preoccupied with the legal battle over Stondon and also by the fact that 'the position of Catholics after 1588 became more and more difficult, and that at this time he was probably occupied with the 'Gradualia' which was essentially a Catholic collection.'

The Revival of Byrd

Thus ended the life of William Byrd, the greatest composer England had produced. The cloud of 'popish recusancy' which hung round him in life would seem to have enwrapped him still closer in death. By the nineteenth century he had become, for every practical purpose, a name in musical history books—the recipient of lip service and little beyond. Barnard (*Selected Church Music*, 1641) printed thirteen of his English anthems and services. By Boyce's time (*Cathedral Music*, 1760–78) the number had dropped to one service and three anthems. The London 'Musical Antiquarian Society' —formed in 1840—started off with the publication, in score, of the five-part Mass and the five-part 'Cantiones' (the latter containing Horsley's now notorious Preface, a monument of pontifical pedantry), but they soon ran out of print and no public performances are on record. The closing years of the century found Byrd represented on one publisher's list by a few madrigals, a service, and a handful of English anthems performed occasionally at a few cathedrals. The same publishers had the courage to issue the Mass for four voices which was produced at the London Oratory under Thomas Wingham

G. E. P. Arkwright had published his scholarly (and now well-known) edition of the 'Songs of Sundry Natures' (in 1892), but at his own expense, as no publisher dared face the risk. Byrd was clearly a drug on the market. When the present writer revived the five-part Mass in 1899 it was printed by a German firm, as the English publishers to whom it was submitted said, quite truly, that there was no market for it. From this edition the Birmingham Festival of 1900 had the courage to give a performance, under Hans Richter, but of only four items out of the six, for the committee said, again quite truly, that the public of that day would not stand more from a composer possessing (as was then said) merely 'an antiquarian interest.' Then, from 1898 for a period of over a quarter of a century, two institutions were responsible for a steady revival of Byrd's music. Public performances were given from MS. copies, as printed ones did not then exist. Their output covered (1) The Masses, (2) two volumes of 'Gradualia,' (3) the volume of five-part 'Cantiones,' (4) the volume (with a few exceptions) of six-part 'Cantiones,' (6) the bulk of the Tallis-Byrd 'Cantiones' of 1575. The work was carried out under difficulties known only to the pioneers who initiated it. Eventually the *Daily Telegraph* and shortly afterwards *The Times* took an active interest in it, with the result that the British Public 'began to sit up and take notice' and to revise its estimate of Byrd. A new public was created, not only for Byrd but for the rest of his contemporaries and predecessors. Publishers no longer found him 'an uncommercial proposition.' Tudor music became a vogue, then a fashionable cult which is only now beginning to show signs of sagging. More than this bare recital of facts it is not for me to give, for reasons that will be obvious.

Byrd's madrigals and songs are now accessible; so is the bulk of his virginal music (including the monumental 'My Ladye Nevell's Booke'); and the bulk of his English and Latin church music; public performances are given all over the country; the B.B.C. has done, and is still doing, its share

in bringing his music into every home. This absolves me
from the necessity of stressing in so short an article Byrd's
pioneer work in giving shape and substances to types of
music that before his time had been formless and chaotic,
and leaves me some space for his Latin music. It is his most
important work; all responsible critics now agree on that
point. It gives the truest insight into his life, character and
habit of mind, but it is in this connection that I have yet to
find an English critic who shows real comprehension of what
it is all about. Some have studied the music deeply and
diligently; they show an artist's reaction to its beauty; they
write intelligently about it as sheer *music*, but when it comes
to the *significance* of it, whether ethical or liturgical, they
'miss the bus.' It is not their fault; it is merely a geographical
accident of birth. The culture into which a man is born and
in which he is bred dominates his life and thought and colours
his outlook, whether he knows the fact or not. The Englishman—whether he calls himself Agnostic or Anglo-Catholic
—has been bred in a Protestant culture; the French Atheist in
a Catholic one. These respective cultures are in their respective blood and bones. But they are as opposite as the poles.
So when it comes to comprehending Byrd's Catholic outlook,
the French Atheist will do so more readily than the Englishman because, however much he may detest Catholicism, he
does *really* understand it; the Englishman only *thinks* he does
and that is all the difference. Moreover it is inborn in the
Englishman, however much he may deny it, that 'religion'
is something loftily remote from his daily grind; consequently,
if he is well-bred, he places any discussion of it on his list of
Things that are Not Done. He becomes uneasy if anyone
refers to it, however casually, in conversation. He sets him
down as a hypocrite or an ass. In nine cases out of ten he is
right. It is at the tenth one that he is 'sunk.' Some perfectly
simple explanation of some perfectly simple issue happens to
be a 'religious' one; so he bolts for the nearest cover immediately it begins and never gets within earshot of the answer.
I ought to add that the devastating qualities I have just

mentioned belong to my own generation. The young generation of to-day, to whom I address myself, is happily free from them and will not misunderstand me when I say that the key to Byrd's character will be found in the 'Gradualia.'

The Clue of the 'Gradualia'

First—on the liturgical side—it resolves itself into musical settings for (a) 'The Proper of the Mass' (that is, Introit, Gradual, Offertory, Communion); (b) other texts which would occur during Mass at special seasons (for example, the Litany at Rogationtide, Holy Saturday and Whitsun Eve, the Passion on Good Friday); (c) Antiphons and Hymns in honour of Our Lady. (The last named are accounted for by the practice, in English collegiate, monastic and cathedral establishments, of following the Mass and Office of each day with the Mass and Office of Our Lady.) The above component parts again resolve themselves into two main divisions —music to Our Lord; music for Our Lady; to the worship of Our Lord as God, in 'The Sacrifice of the Mass,' and to the honour of Our Lady as His earthly mother, in 'The Divine Office.'

(May I remind twentieth-century readers that I am here using the common terminology of Byrd's day and not indulging in pietistic expressions of my own?)

Secondly, it is noteworthy that no other composer, not even Palestrina, ever attempted so crystallised a presentation of this idea—the Mass the sun and centre; the Office of B.V.M. a constellation circling round it. Palestrina wrote more Masses, Motets and Hymns B.V.M., but neither he nor anyone else conceived the idea of moulding them into an architectural structure like this. Byrd must have had some reason for standing alone among composers in rearing a challenging monument to the Mass in a form and on a scale never attempted before or since.

Thirdly, if we can only rid ourselves of the popular habit of reading history backwards, his reason is not far to seek.

The times were critical. Europe was engaged in a deadly struggle. In England no man's life was safe. Whatever political shapes it might take, the struggle centred round the Mass and all that it implied. In the words of the late Augustine Birrell—'It was the Mass that mattered; it was the Mass that made the difference.' In Byrd's day you either loved or hated the Mass, but you could not remain indifferent to it. Englishmen of Byrd's time had seen so many religious changes that they were not inclined to believe in the permanence of any one of them. English Catholics still looked hopefully to the future—'waiting for a day' they called it—but I cannot think that Byrd was under any illusions. He saw deeper than his fellows. It has been suggested that he prepared his 'Gradualia' against the day when the old religion would return with its old splendour. Against that we must put the practical difficulty that 'The Proper of the Mass' had never been (and was never likely to be) sung with such elaboration as Byrd gave to it. I prefer to believe that this work, to which he devoted the last years of his life, was in the nature of a declaration of the faith that was in him; a dedication of his powers at their ripest to the Mass, which was to him 'the thing that mattered; the thing that made the difference.' His volumes of Motets are all supplementary to that central rite with one exception, the five-part 'Cantiones' of 1589.

Though any of these could be used as Motets at Mass, their tone is unmistakably intimate and personal. It requires no effort of the imagination to see in their poignant grief the outpouring of a troubled soul; the cause of his distress is unmistakable. His lament over Sion wasted and laid low, his passionate cry *Veni Domine; noli tardare, et libera populum tuum* leave no doubt of what the passing of the old religion meant to him. Even the calm poise and balance of the All Saints' motet and the jubilant outbursts of the Christmas and Easter ones are all in the picture, provided one does not (as I said before) read history backwards. It is noteworthy that while Byrd's other motets are drawn from liturgical sources, most of these are taken from current books of private devotions; hence the intimacy of both words and music.

The 'Gradualia' would offer many more points for comment (and of interest to the general reader), did space permit. Since that is not possible, one ought perhaps to say that it will not disclose its inmost self to the critic who approaches it from the modern viewpoint or who interprets it according to the standards of to-day. I have seen in print some descriptions of it that bristle with 'howlers' on elementary points which a little liturgical knowledge would have rendered impossible.

I hope I may be forgiven if I end on a personal note. As I read in turn Byrd's various Prefaces I began to feel myself in a strangely familiar atmosphere. Here—thought I—are the same turns of speech; here is the same quaint gravity, the same shrewd judgment, the same quiet humour, that are met in the writings of the old English mystics. Here—I thought—is one with the same spiritual outlook, the same grave courtesy, the same English reticence and restraint in the presence of high matters. Here, in intellect, in love of beauty, in love of country, in sincerity of heart is one in the same fellowship with Hugh of Avalon, Adam of Dryburgh, Nicholas Love, Julian of Norwich, Walter Hilton, Stephen Harding, John Fisher, Thomas More, the anonymous authors of *Eden's Fourfold River* and the rest of that goodly company who showed the world that the truest mysticism postulates the truest *sanity*.

This dawning knowledge threw a new light, for me at least, both on the man and on the music that was a part of him. He appealed to me (again, I speak only for myself) as the true mystic, particularly in his approach to mundane affairs. His secular music is luminous in that regard.

Your true mystic is a man of vision (not *visions* as popular belief would have it), and I regard Byrd as none the less a mystic because to that quality he added yet another, which the pietist has a habit of belittling, but which is really one of the jewels in the mystic's crown—he was very, very *human*.

BIBLIOGRAPHY

ANDREWS, HILDA: *Introduction and Notes in 'My Ladye Nevells Booke.'* 63s. (Curwen, 1906.)

FELLOWES, EDMUND H.: *William Byrd: A Short Account of his Life and Work.* 2nd edition. 7s. 6d. (Oxford University Press, 1928.)

GLYN, MARGARET H.: *Elizabethan Music and Composers.* 10s. (Reeves, 1934.)

HOWES, FRANK: *William Byrd.* 7s. 6d. (Kegan Paul, 1928.)

CHRISTOPH WILLIBALD GLUCK

BORN 14 July 1714   DIED 15 November 1787

By Martin Du Pré Cooper

Family Origins—Kommotau, Prague and Vienna

Gluck was born at Weidenwang in the Upper Palatinate. Weidenwang lies between Bayreuth and Karlovy Vary (Karlsbad), on the Czech side of the former German-Czech frontier, and Gluck's family was probably more Czech than German. The name Gluck appeared in many different spellings during the composer's lifetime: Kluck, Kluckh and Kluk are all found, and of these *Kluk* is Czech beyond a doubt, for it is a word in the ordinary language, meaning boy or fellow. But in the eighteenth century the nationalities united under the Austro-Hungarian Empire were less conscious than later of their differences from the central Teutonic race that ruled them from Vienna, and more anxious to emphasise their connection with this race, more advanced culturally and politically more recognised than their own. So that the Hungarians, Czechs, Croats and Italians, by whom the Empire was to a great extent administered, were prouder of their connection with Vienna and Viennese culture and brilliance than of the ties of race and blood for which they came, a hundred years later, to fight so passionately. Gluck's family and Gluck himself probably felt themselves primarily members of the Empire and, as such, Germans. It would be only secondarily that they were aware of belonging to a Slav branch of the Empire; of the various implications and potentialities—emotional or political—of their Slav blood they were probably not at all conscious.

Gluck's father was a keeper by profession. In 1717 he moved to Neuschloss, in the north of the old Bohemia, to a post on the estates of the Prince Kaunitz, and a few years later to the Lobkowitz estates at Eisenberg. Up to the age of twelve, then, the child Gluck lived an absolutely rural life, running wild—and, according to his own account, often barefoot—in the forests and rolling countryside of his home. But in 1726 it was time for him to go to school, and he was sent off to the Jesuit seminary at Kommotau, the nearest town to Eisenberg, where he spent the next six years. Very little is known, naturally enough, of these years at Kommotau, but it is certain that Gluck learned to play both the piano and the organ there, and when he moved to Prague in 1732 it was to study music. For a time he read philosophy too, but before long the allowance made him by his father was discontinued and he was forced to support himself by giving lessons in singing and 'cello-playing. He sang and played at the Teinkirche in Prague, where he was under the direction of Černohorski, a good musician who had spent many years in Italy and had had the great Tartini as a pupil. Černohorski was thus the first link between Gluck and the larger musical world and almost certainly the first musical personality in the boy's life. For the Kommotau Jesuits, though doubtless efficient and conscientious, could probably do no more than give him a solid academic training in the rudiments of music. What holidays Gluck had, he spent in the neighbourhood of Prague and in the larger towns of Bohemia, earning his keep by giving 'cello-recitals, for which he was generally paid in kind. Regular study can have played almost no part in his life at this time. Yet he must have had a certain proficiency both as singer and instrumentalist, for it was thanks to his powers of performance that he finally managed to lever himself out of this small provincial world and to make the acquaintance of international musical life. In 1736 he left Prague for Vienna where, as the gifted son of a retainer, he was received into the Lobkowitz household. It was here that the Prince Melzi heard him sing and play, and being a rich man who patronised the arts and kept a private orchestra of his own, he asked Gluck to join it. Gluck accepted and left Vienna the next year for Milan.

Milan and Sammartini—First Operas

He was probably callow enough when he arrived in Milan. He had composed nothing, so far as is known, and the first regular forming of his musical personality began here; it is therefore not strange that Italian music should have remained to the end of his life one of the strongest influences on his musical idiom. On his arrival he was put to school with Giambattista Sammartini, the most distinguished teacher and composer in the town, a man with a vivacious musical imagination, not afraid to experiment in instrumental music at a time when the instrumental style was still young. It was a misfortune that Sammartini's originality should have been wasted on a pupil who never possessed the purely musical faculty necessary for the writing of instrumental music and would have profited more from the vocal training which a less original teacher would probably have given him. Exactly what he studied with Sammartini is a mystery, for Gluck remained to the end of his life a clumsy craftsman in the ordinary grammar of musical language. Musical beauty and elaboration for their own sakes never meant anything to him, and he probably assimilated only so much of Sammartini's teaching as was necessary to him for the expression of the more literary and dramatic ideals of which he later became the exponent. After four years' study he produced his first opera, 'Artaserse,' at Milan in December, 1741. It must have had a certain success, as Gluck was commissioned to write a 'Demetrio' the next year for Venice and a second opera, 'Demofoonte,' for Milan. In the next two years he produced five operas, performed in Venice, Milan and Turin, and contributed to two·pasticci. These pasticci were potpourris composed of a number of favourite airs taken from the operas of different composers, with a few newly composed numbers added and possibly a new text. They were naturally very popular, for the public wanted then, as now, the catchiest tunes of the year combined in one evening's entertainment and was little concerned with relevance or dramatic verity. Gluck's chief concern during these eight years in Italy was to catch the popular taste and to ensure himself a large number of engagements. The music he wrote was the conventional music of the Italian *opera seria*, a rather stiff artistic form consisting of formal arias accompanied by the orchestra, interspersed with recitative accompanied on the harpsichord. There is very little individuality about any of these early works of Gluck, and it is possible that he might have settled permanently in Italy, adopted Italian habits and musical standards, and ended his life as a conventional composer of second-rate Italian music, had he not received an invitation from the Haymarket Theatre in London and been taken off to England by his first patron, the Prince Lobkowitz. He left Milan in 1745 and travelled through Paris to London.

England—Dresden and Copenhagen

It was an unfortunate moment to arrive in England; after the Jacobite rising, feeling was strong against the Catholic Church, and the Opera had had to be closed for fear of demonstrations against the singers who, as Italians, were known to be Catholics. However, on 7th January, 1746, Gluck gave 'La Caduta dei Giganti' or 'The Fall of the Giants,' a *pasticcio* of his own works, in which the giants were of course symbolical of the defeated Jacobites. On 4th March he produced a second *pasticcio*, 'Artamene': and towards the end of April he gave two concerts on the *verrillon* or glass-harmonica. The accounts of his success in London vary. There are the well-known stories of Handel saying that Gluck knew no more of counterpoint than his cook did, advising him to take less trouble for English audiences and to write music which sounded the big drum—it was the only kind they understood. Dr. Burney, on the other hand, blames the singers for the comparative failure of 'La Caduta' and speaks of Gluck as a promising composer. In any case the importance of Gluck's visit to London does not lie in his active productions, whose merit was on any showing small, but rather to the fact that here he made the acquaintance of Handel's music. It was an acquaintance that quickly ripened into a deep admiration, Gluck declaring to the end of his life that Handel was his favourite composer and proving his sincerity by approximating, more and more, as he grew older, to the breadth, simplicity and vigour of Handel's style.

Prague and Vienna Again—Marriage

Gluck left England in May, 1746, and is not heard of again until thirteen months later, when he was at Dresden for a performance of his 'Nozze d'Ercole e d'Ebe'—a mythological piece written to celebrate a royal wedding. He may have spent the summer and autumn of 1746 travelling in South Germany and Austria with the Mingotti theatrical troupe which performed the 'Nozze d'Ercole' at Dresden, but there is no definite proof that he did. Some time between June, 1747, and May, 1748—when Gluck appears in Vienna again with his first great success, the opera 'Semiramide Riconosciuta'—his father died and Gluck seems to have gone home to sell a small shop and property left to him. He was back with the Mingotti troupe in the October of 1748, this time in Hamburg; from there the whole company set out in November for Copenhagen. During the five months Gluck spent with the company in Denmark he was ill, but he managed to give two of his verrillon concerts and to compose an opera, 'La Contesa dei Numi,' which was performed by the company on 9th April, to celebrate the birth of the Prince Christian.

The Mingotti season in Copenhagen ended on 23rd April and Gluck returned to Vienna, where we next hear of him as engaged to marry Marianne Pergin, the daughter of a rich Viennese merchant, who disapproved of Gluck and would not be persuaded by his wife into allowing the marriage. Gluck left Vienna—for Italy, according to his earliest biographers, who say that he gave his opera 'Telemacco' at Rome in 1750. On the other hand it is known that Gluck only once gave an opera in Rome—the 'Antigono' of 1756—and it is almost certain that 'Telemacco' was composed considerably later. It is far more likely that Gluck was in Prague, where his opera 'Ezio' was given during the carnival of 1750. In September of this year old Herr Pergin died and, on the 15th, Gluck was married to Marianne and settled down to live with her in her mother's house. His prospects were not very bright. He was thirty-six years old and had no regular position, but depended entirely on chance engagements—and now on his wife's comfortable income, as her father had probably foreseen. However, he was commissioned to write another opera, 'Issipile,' for Prague during the carnival of 1752, and 'La Clemenza di Tito' for Naples in the autumn of the same year. Naples had been the centre of the operatic world ever since the beginning of the century, when Alessandro Scarlatti had made it famous, and in 1752 it was still a great honour for a foreigner to be asked to write a work for the Naples Opera. 'La Clemenza di Tito' won Gluck golden opinions among the Neapolitans, and a single air from the opera—'Se mai senti spirarti sul petto'—sung by the great Caffarelli, became so famous that it was the direct means of getting Gluck a post when he returned to Vienna in December. This post was Kapellmeister to the Prince of Sachsen-Hildburghausen.

An Imperial Patron

For the next two years Gluck's life was uneventful. He lived with his wife in her mother's house, composing and arranging for the Prince's private orchestra many of his airs and symphonies, according to Dittersdorf, who was a member of the orchestra and a favourite of Gluck. It was not

until the autumn of 1754 that anything occurred to interrupt
the monotony of this life.   In September of this year Gluck's
patron invited the Empress Maria Theresa to visit him at his
country estate of Schlosshof, and Gluck was commissioned
to write an opera for the occasion.   'Le Cinesi,' a light piece
by Metastasio, the favourite poet of the day, was chosen;
the production of it was so lavish, the music apparently so
charming to the Empress, that she appointed Gluck on the
spot to the post of Kapellmeister for the opera at the Court
Theatre.   This was one of the most important musical posts
in Vienna and brought Gluck into contact with all the most
liberal and cultured elements of Society, as well as with the
best artists of the day.   For the next seven years (1754–61)
he was busy, not only writing French comedies and occasional Italian operas for Court functions, but also making up
for the defects of his early education, learning French and
studying the classics.   In 1753 a Count Durazzo had been
appointed Intendant of the Opera, and in him Gluck found a
highly cultured and sympathetic friend.   Some of the most
famous artistic figures of the time were in Vienna during these
years—amongst them the dancer Gasparo Angiolini,
Noverre's rival, and the scene-painter Quaglio, with both
of whom Gluck became intimate.   In 1756 he received a
commission from Rome, where he went in February to
produce his 'Antigono.'   There he was under the patronage
of the Cardinal Albani, later the patron of Winckelmann;
whether Gluck and Winckelmann actually met or not, it is
impossible that the Cardinal's wonderful collections of
antiques should have had no influence on Gluck.   They
must rather have helped to form and add to his already
marked taste for the civilisation and mythology of the
ancient world.

Calzabigi and Vienna

In 1761 appeared the first fruit of Gluck's collaboration with
Gasparo Angiolini, the ballet 'Don Juan,' and in the following

year 'Orfeo,' the music by Gluck, scenery by Quaglio, ballets by Angiolini, text by Ranieri Calzabigi. This Ranieri Calzabigi was an exact contemporary of Gluck, having been born in 1714 at Leghorn. After a rather stormy career as diplomatic attaché at Naples and in Paris he came to Vienna in 1761 and at once took his place in the society of cultured and liberal artists connected with Durazzo and the Court Theatre. 'Orfeo' created a sensation for two reasons. The large rôle played by the chorus in the first two acts was a break with the practice of contemporary Italian opera, and the weakening of the distinction between recitative and air, a general tendency for the whole poem to approximate to a single type of impassioned but only semi-formal declamation, cut at the root-principle of the old opera. The recitatives, too, were accompanied for the first time by the orchestra instead of by the harpsichord, thus making a homogeneous whole of a form which had hitherto been divided between two quite distinct kinds of tone-colour. After their first surprise at these innovations, the Viennese Court and Society took enthusiastically to the work, and Gluck probably made a comfortable sum of money out of it. For in the next year (1763) he and his wife moved from his mother-in-law's house to their own, at the corner of the Kärntnerstrasse and the Walfischgasse, and here they remained for the next six years. In the spring Gluck went to Bologna to produce his 'Trionfo di Clelia,' an opera commissioned for the opening of the new theatre. He took with him the young Dittersdorf, who has left an interesting account of the journey in his autobiography. The two travelled to Venice with a young prima donna, with whom Gluck enjoyed flirting. In Bologna itself there were two state visits to be paid—the one to the Padre Martini, the most learned musical historian and theoretician in Europe, the other to Farinelli, the famous singer who had retired to Bologna. Gluck had planned to return to Vienna by slow stages, sightseeing on the way, but his plans were put out by a sudden message bidding him hurry home to help in the preparations for the coronation of the

Archduke Joseph as King of the Romans, which took place early the next year in Frankfurt.

'Alceste'—Success in Vienna

In the December of 1763 Gluck's single comic opera, 'The Pilgrims of Mecca' was performed in Vienna. The next year Durazzo resigned from his post as Intendant of the Court Theatre and Gluck followed him, after holding his post ten years. He kept his position as singing-master to the royal family, however, and during the year he produced a small opera at Schönbrunn, 'Il Parnasso Confuso,' with a cast consisting entirely of royalties. In January 1765, 'Telemacco' was produced in Vienna and was followed the next day by a new ballet in which Gluck had again collaborated with Angiolini, 'Semiramide.' For the year 1766 we have no record of Gluck's activities, and it is likely that he was quietly composing the major work with which he startled Vienna in the following year. In the spring of 1767 he was at Florence for the production of his 'Prologo,' a cantata written to celebrate the birth of a son to the reigning Duke of Tuscany. Back in Vienna, it was not until December that he finally produced 'Alceste,' the work which really earned him the name of reformer of the opera. In his preface to the score he wrote '. . . I have thought it necessary to reduce music to its true function, which is that of seconding poetry in the expression of sentiments and dramatic situations of a story, neither interrupting the action nor detracting from its vividness by useless and superfluous ornament. . . . Further I have thought that my greatest efforts should be directed to the search for beauty in simplicity. I have avoided a display of difficulty at the expense of clarity, and have valued the discovery of any novelty only so far as it was naturally suggested by the situation or necessary to the expression. There is no academic rule which I have not willingly sacrificed to dramatic effect.' In the preface to his 'Paris and Helen,' which was given three years later in Vienna, he makes

c

his objective still plainer. 'I only decided to publish the music of "Alceste,"' he writes, 'in the hope of finding imitators. I thought that these disciples, continuing my efforts and encouraged by an enlightened public, would use all their energies to destroy the abuses from which Italian art is suffering and to raise this same art to a higher level. My idea has proved vain: I deplore the fact. . . . I do not expect my "Paris" to be any more successful than my "Alceste."' Yet when he was asked to write a 'Feste d'Apollo' for Parma in 1769, he was shrewd enough to forget his high principles and to write the kind of showy singers' music that he knew an Italian audience appreciated. He was not going to cast his pearls before swine—or risk a refusal of his fee.

But in Vienna he was the doyen of the musical world. He had moved in 1768 to a large and fashionable house in the Rennweg, where he used to entertain in a grand style. Dr. Burney, visiting Vienna in 1772, was invited there by Gluck, whom he had met at the English ambassador's house, and was delighted by the performance of Gluck's music given by the composer himself and his niece, Marianne Heller, whom he had adopted. She had a beautiful voice, despite her youth (she was only thirteen), and Dr. Burney was delighted with her singing of Alceste and portions of Gluck's new opera, 'Iphigénie en Aulide,' which he was writing for Paris. The libretto was drawn from Racine's tragedy and had been written by an attaché at the French Embassy in Vienna, the Bailly du Roullet. Marie Antoinette, the wife of the then Dauphin, had been a pupil of Gluck, and he contrived to get himself invited to Paris on the most favourable terms for the production of his opera. He left Vienna in the late summer of 1773, accompanied by his wife and niece: as soon as he arrived in Paris, rehearsals began. They lasted six months. For although Gluck had considered the different traditions of the French opera in writing his new work, he found many of the existing conditions of performance intolerable, and he did not rest until they were altered to suit him.

'Iphigénie en Aulide'—Paris and Piccinni

'Iphigénie en Aulide' was given before a packed house on 19th April, 1776. It was a success. But although Gluck had been tactful enough to make his first appearance in Paris with a libretto drawn from Racine and to claim to base his operatic method on that of Lully, he was bound to arouse opposition. There was the literary world first of all, headed by Rousseau, which believed only in Italian music and thought that a French text damned a work in advance. Then there were the faithful admirers of Lully and Rameau, who were sure to resent any new style, even though it might retain and develop all that was most valuable in the old, as Gluck could claim to do. Finally Paris was always in need of some new party issue, some question—it mattered little whether it was religious, intellectual or artistic—on which society could take sides, as a form of mental and social drug to distract attention from the growing discontent of all but the very few. For Gluck arrived in Paris less than twenty years before the revolution and the famous quarrel which arose over his music was not a musical dispute so much as a journalists' racket.

On 2nd August, 1774, Gluck followed 'Iphigénie' with a new version of 'Orfeo,' specially made for the French stage. And when he left Paris in the following February to return to Vienna he took two libretti by Quinault which the Opera had asked him to set. These were 'Roland' and 'Armide,' both of which had been set by Lully. But the enemies he left behind him were powerful and their leaders, Marmontel and Caraccioli, the Neapolitan ambassador, were not idle. They decided that their best plan was to get hold of a rival composer to put up against Gluck, and for this purpose they chose an Italian, Niccolò Piccinni, whom they commissioned to set the same 'Roland' that Gluck was engaged on. However, no sooner had Gluck got wind of this ruse than he tore up all the music that he had written for 'Roland' and confined himself to the composition of 'Armide.' He returned to Paris in February 1776 to produce a new French version of his 'Alceste.' But he only stayed a few months, for on 22nd April, the day before the Paris performance of 'Alceste,' his beloved niece Marianne died of smallpox in Vienna. Although Frau Gluck did her best to console him for the loss of his 'little nightingale,' as he used to call her, the applause he won from 'Alceste' meant little to him and he returned to Vienna sad and depressed, to complete 'Armide.' This was produced in September 1777, under Gluck's direction, and was at first not a great success. Before Gluck returned to Vienna this time, Berton, director of the Opera, arranged that he should meet Piccinni at a small dinner-party. The two rivals got on excellently, Gluck quite at his ease, talking cynically about the French and maliciously delighted when Piccinni began naïvely to boast about the short time he needed for composition. His 'Roland,' which was given in January 1778, was a great success, much to its nervous composer's astonishment.

Back to Vienna—Last Years

Gluck spent nearly a year in Vienna on the composition of his last great work, the 'Iphigénie en Tauride' by Guillard, which was finally given, after five months' rehearsing, on 18th May, 1778. It had an immediate success, a success which crowned and closed Gluck's career as a composer. He had the misfortune, however, to produce another small work in Paris before he left. This was 'Echo et Narcisse,' which was given on 24th September and called forth a stream of parodies, epigrams and pasquinades. Gluck was furious and more than ever determined to leave Paris by the fact that he was only beginning to recover his strength after the first of a series of apoplectic fits, which finally caused his death.

Following his first success in Paris he had been appointed Maria Theresa's Chamber-Composer, and he now returned to Vienna to this office, which required very little of him and brought in a more than comfortable salary. Gluck was

sixty-five years old and no longer strong in health. He had
accumulated enough money to be able to indulge his taste
for grand entertainment, a large house like a nobleman's
and expensive clothes. But he did not entirely give up
composition. He refused a request for an opera for Naples
in 1783, feeling that he no longer had the power of concen-
tration necessary for the construction of a large work. Instead he busied himself with his settings of Klopstock's Odes,
which he had begun as early as 1772, and with helping his
pupil Salieri (the future master of Beethoven and Schubert),
who was composing a cantata on the Last Judgment. He
followed musical events in Vienna with great interest, and
was enthusiastic over Mozart's 'Entführung' when it was
produced in 1782. He had missed seeing Mozart in Paris,
but made his acquaintance now and twice asked him and his
wife to dinner, once in August 1782 and again in March 1783.
He was still clear-brained and even witty at this time: but
three years later, when Salieri came to say good-bye to him
before leaving for Paris, he could only mumble a few phrases
in a hotch-potch of languages. 'Ainsi, mon cher ami . . .
Lei parte domani per Parigi . . . je vous souhaite . . . di
cuore un bon voyage . . . Sie gehen in eine Stadt, wo man die
fremden Künstler schätzt . . . e Lei farà onore . . . ich zweifle
nicht. . . . Ci scriva, mais bien souvent.'

His death occurred on 15th November, 1787. Left alone
with two friends from Paris, whom he had been entertaining
to lunch, Gluck insisted on drinking a glass of liqueur strictly
forbidden him by the doctor, and this brought on a final
apoplectic fit an hour later, while he was out for his afternoon
drive. He never recovered consciousness, but died the same
evening and was buried two days later at the Matzleinsdorf
cemetery, in a simple grave with this inscription:

> Here lies a forthright German man.
> A zealous Christian. A faithful husband.
> CHRISTOPH RITTER GLUCK.
> Great master of the mighty art of music.

His Will, beyond the leaving of all his property to his wife, was a short and enigmatic one. 'I leave to the Poor House, 1 florin: to the General Hospital, 1 florin: to the Town Hospital, 1 florin: to the High School, 1 florin: in all four florins.' His income from the Paris Opera alone was estimated at little less than 1,000,000 livres.

The Man and the Musician

Gluck's physical appearance tallied exactly with his peasant origin—large, big-boned, with a broad, open face and a florid, pock-marked complexion. His excellent business sense, too —his ability to drive a good bargain and his meanness with the money he amassed—are regular peasant traits, while the alternate obsequiousness and braggadocio of his manner, his inability to accept any form of hostile criticism, or to admit himself mistaken, are all marks of a man who has risen into a class where he does not feel sure of himself. Defending himself against Rousseau's allegation of an anachronism in 'Paris and Helen,' he took refuge in the most laughable evasion rather than admit himself mistaken on a point of history—for Rousseau did not question the artistic effect, which was the only point Gluck need have felt himself obliged to uphold. Enthusiastic, vigorous and direct like his music, Gluck was a typical self-made man, who had learnt early in his career that anyone determined to do well for himself cannot afford to think of much besides his own interests. He was by no means the intransigeant idealist painted by some of his biographers, believing rather that with a little cleverness he could have the best of both worlds. In actual fact he did contrive to create great and revolutionary works of art and at the same time to be paid far more lavishly for them than the rest of his contemporaries, who were frankly concerned with the production of what the public wanted.

Gluck has had comparatively little influence on the history of music. Admired by most composers, he has been imitated by none, and his works are very seldom performed. He epitomised the best of the age in which he lived, but he very seldom sounded a really prophetic note, his method being far more revolutionary than his actual idiom. He was a child of the German *Aufklärung*, but hardly touched by the *Sturm und Drang* which left their trace in the works of Haydn and Mozart. The twentieth century has not a great deal to learn from Gluck musically, and Debussy even went so far as to attack him for his stiff and heavily accentuated treatment of the French language, which, it is true, only a foreigner could have conceived. But as a dramatist and a poet Gluck will not die so easily. Standing alone at the end of a period of cultural history and gathering together the best elements in the art of his time in order to make a new use of them, Gluck inevitably predicted, and to a certain extent influenced, the future of lyric drama, contriving at least some part of that immortality of which he was so pathetically assured in his lifetime.

BIBLIOGRAPHY

AREND, MAX: *Gluck; eine Biographie.* (Berlin and Leipzig, 1921.)
COOPER, MARTIN DU PRÉ: *Gluck.* 12s. 6d. (Chatto & Windus, 1935.)
NEWMAN, ERNEST: *Gluck and the Opera.* O.P. (Dobell, 1895.)

GEORGE FREDERICK
HANDEL

BORN 23 February 1685   DIED 14 April 1759

By W. McNaught

Boyhood

In the Middle Ages the town of Halle in Saxony was a centre
of aristocratic life, culture and gaiety. At the end of the
Thirty Years' War political changes caused its · resident
nobility to withdraw to a neighbouring capital, and by the
end of the seventeenth century Halle had settled down to a
comparatively obscure provincial existence. It remained,
however, a town of sufficient importance for its leading
citizens to take some pride in their standing. One of these
citizens was Georg Handel (1622–97), the composer's father.
A younger son in a family of coppersmiths, he had taken up
the profession of barber-surgeon and had risen in it to the
foremost position in Halle. When he was over sixty years
old he took a second wife, Dorothea, *née* Taust. Their first
child died. The second was Georg Friederich Handel.*

The story of the child's first artistic exploit cannot be
passed over, for it is recorded in oils and can be bought on
many a picture-postcard. The infant Handel had so yearned
for a keyboard that the indulgent mother smuggled a clavichord into the garret; tinkling sounds after bed-time brought
a paternal raid upon the unofficial music-room, and the infant
was forbidden to play any more at being a musician. Whether

* In his later years the composer wrote his second name as Frideric.
To the English people he was always George Frederick Handel.

the story be true or false, the barber-surgeon's opposition
to musical projects is authentic and quite intelligible. Having
risen himself far above his family beginnings, he looked
forward to a further elevation on the part of his offspring,
and to that end had chosen the study of the law. For one
of his family to become a musician would be in his eyes a
fall to a lower depth than the ancestral copper-beating.
According to the notions of the time he was right, for the
musical profession had not then won its independence and
was destined not to do so until the nineteenth century.
George Handel did not wish his son to become a lackey.
The next incident softens the picture of parental sternness.
It appears that at the age of seven the young Handel accompanied his father on a journey to Wiessenfels, where the
Duke of Saxony then resided, and was so far permitted to
show off his talent that the Duke heard him play on the
chapel organ. The Duke interceded for the young genius,
with the result that the boy thenceforward received lessons
from Zachow, the organist at the Liebfrauenkirche in Halle.
Zachow appears to have been a well-founded musician and
his tuition rigorous and thorough. The lessons continued
for three years, and the fame of the boy's precocity as a player
began to spread.

The next episode is one of which the chronicles speak
vaguely. Handel was taken to Berlin, with no other dis-
coverable object than that of displaying his musical talent.
According to the generally accepted account the journey
took place in 1696, the year before Georg Handel's death.
It does not follow that the old man had entirely relented in
his opposition to a musical career, for he refused an offer to
send young Handel to Italy and ordered him back from
Berlin. The boy-virtuoso had been the sensation of the hour
at the Electoral Court, and probably his father was more
discerning than tyrannical in bringing him back to his studies.
On returning to Halle, young Handel found himself at the
death-bed of his father, a remote, mysterious and forbidding
man with whom he could never have been on terms of

affection. His sense of duty kept him some years to his general studies, but soon after his entry at the university his fame called him to a musician's task.

The post of organist to the Cathedral at the Moritzburg, the former residence of archbishops and dukes, became vacant. Though the church was Calvinist and Handel was a Lutheran he was given the appointment, and he held it for over a year. From this time we hear no more of university and legal studies. Handel was set upon a musical career. In search of it he left Halle in the summer of 1703, to return only for occasional visits when his professional journeys gave him the opportunity and left him the time.

At Hamburg

His first journey was to Hamburg, where he was soon engaged as a second violin in the orchestra at the opera house. Hamburg had at this time taken the lead of Berlin as a musical centre. It had emerged from the troubles of the seventeenth century a prosperous and gay commercial city. Its opera house plays an important part in musical history as the last stronghold to resist the invasion of Italian fashions. That it held out as long as it did was mainly due to Reinhard Keiser (1673–1739), who directed the theatre from 1694 and wrote over a hundred operas in the German tradition. It was under Keiser that Handel found employment. At the same time he formed a useful friendship with the versatile and volatile Johann Mattheson (1681–1764), a musician who made his chief mark in the world by his varied talents as a man. It was owing to Mattheson's offices that Handel was able to maintain himself by teaching and to find his feet in the musical circle of Hamburg.

His gradually increasing repute gave him access to the church organs of the city, and from this it came about that his first large-scale composition was written for the church and not for the theatre. The music of Handel's 'Passion of

St. John' is negligible in the light of his later works, but, with Mozart alone excepted, it is probably the best work extant by a composer of nineteen. It was, however, soon to be outclassed by Handel's first opera. Keiser, too taken up by business or self-indulgence to set a libretto called *Almira*, passed it to Handel, who wrote the music in haste. The opera was produced early in 1705 and became the success of the season. It had a nonsensical plot and it was sung in two languages—Italian for the formal arias, German for the recitative. But it displayed a freshness and accomplishment that were new to Hamburg and can still be recognised as bearing the authentic touch of the master. Handel's success drew upon him the enmity of Keiser and brought out the falseness, of which Handel had already had proof, of Mattheson's friendship. This unstable character does not play an important part in Handel's life, but he figures prominently in Handel's biography, for his written reminiscences, unreliable as they are, give us some useful clues to the Hamburg period; and moreover he narrowly escaped doing bodily injury to Handel in a duel. During the autumn of 1704 Mattheson was singing the tenor part in 'Cleopatra,' his own opera. After his demise on the stage it was his custom to go into the orchestra and direct the remainder of the performance at the harpsichord. Handel, as harpsichordist, acquiesced in this arrangement for some time, but one evening suddenly refused to give up his place. The resulting quarrel, enacted in full view of the public, led to a duel in which Mattheson's sword broke on one of Handel's buttons. The quarrel was made up, but in the following year Handel's successes worked on Mattheson's jealousy, and there was no peace in their friendship. Later on, in a book of contemporary biographies, Mattheson wrote slightingly of Handel, possibly in offence at Handel's refusal in 1719 to contribute an autobiographical chapter. Handel's second opera was 'Nero.' It failed and has been lost. Operatic life in Hamburg was degenerating under Keiser's mismanagement, and Handel found other ways of maintaining himself.

Italy

Little is known of his last years in Hamburg beyond the
fact that he made the acquaintance of Giovanni Gastone dei
Medici, the second son of Cosmo III, Duke of Tuscany.
This prince was a notorious rake whose only redeeming
feature in the eyes of history was his fondness for music.
It was presumably this alone that prompted an upright and
clean-living man like Handel to make friends with a libertine.
The prince talked to Handel of Italian music, invited him to
Italy, and offered to pay the expenses of the journey.   Handel
declined, no doubt because he lacked faith in the paymaster,
and possibly because he had not yet learnt to admire the
Italian style of music.   He was still a German musician, even
his opera 'Almira,' with all its Italian element, being more
German than Italian.   Yet in those days a man of culture
could not for long remain indifferent to the call of Italy,
especially if he were a musician.

During the seventeenth century, Italy led the world in the
art of music.   In England the bright flame of Purcell shone
alone for a moment; France had little to show but the ballet-
operas of Lulli; in Germany a scattered school of organists
nourished the chorale and prepared the way for Bach.   But
in Italy almost the whole of modern music was taking shape.
Opera and oratorio, at first scarcely distinguishable, grew in
dignity and force under Cavalli and Carissimi, and from their
songs sprang almost the whole of vocal music, apart from the
church, until the time of Schubert; Corelli set the standard
of violin-playing for the future and established the instrumental form that was destined to develop into the sonata;
harpsichord music still awaited its master, but Italy was to
produce him; at Rome, Frescobaldi was the greatest of the
early organists, and grouped about the Sistine Chapel were
the institutions of a school of church music as eternal as the
city itself.   At the time when Handel was turning his eyes
to the south, the Arcadian Academy at Rome had among its
members Corelli, Pasquini and the most famous composer of

the time, Alessandro Scarlatti. Moreover, apart from the activity of its composers, Italy was the land where music was most eagerly cultivated and where its practice was held in highest esteem. In all countries the continuance of music depended largely upon the private establishments—whether chapels, theatres, or *salons*—maintained by the richer aristocracy. In Italy such establishments were more numerous and more bountifully upheld than elsewhere. Patronage of music was more liberal of mind as well as of purse. Moreover, Italy was rich in cities of musical renown: Florence, Rome, Naples, Venice—each was a metropolis for the musician, and each in turn must our wandering Saxon needs visit.

Italian Journey

The promise of such a land was irresistible to Handel the adventurer. Such a term does not come amiss to him at this stage, for it is only our later knowledge that gives a warrant to his exploits. It was an intrepid and self-reliant young man who set out across Europe with no money but what he had saved from a teacher's fees, with no knowledge of how he was to add to it, with no friends in the country to which he was going, except a possibly fickle prince of dubious character, and with only a smattering, if that, of the language. Apart from what provision he had in the form of letters of recommendation and his own native sagacity, Handel's prospects were those of a strolling player.

Bold and speculative as the venture was, Handel made a success of it. He must have been a man whose sterling character and determination revealed themselves in his manner and intercourse. And he must have had a large stock of native gumption. It could only have been such qualities, aiding and abetting his musical talent, that gained him an entry and a personal standing among the aristocrats and musical leaders of Italy and sustained him amid the difficulties and no doubt the jealousies that would beset a foreigner.

The steps of his approach to the high places we do not know; we know only that one after another the most influential magnates of the musical world took him under their protection.

His first halting place was Florence, where he was received in the late summer or autumn of 1706 by Prince Ferdinand of Tuscany, the elder brother of Giovanni Gastone. He next appears at Rome in January, 1707, one of the few established dates in the chronology of his Italian years.* At Rome the Pope had laid an interdict upon opera, so Handel did as the Romans did and wrote music for the church. The reputation he immediately won by his 'Dixit Dominus' and other works, and by his playing an organ and harpsichord, quickly gained him the entry into the highest circle of art and patronage. Some time in 1707 he appears to have gone to Florence, where his first Italian opera 'Rodrigo' was performed under the patronage of Prince Ferdinand. He is next heard of in Venice, where he seems to have spent some months late in 1707. Of this visit scarcely anything is on record but three notable friendships. One, with Domenico Scarlatti, endured for many years and was afterwards renewed in London. The second was with Prince Ernest of Hanover, a younger brother of the Elector George who was afterwards to be King George of England. By inviting Handel to come to Hanover at the end of his Italian tour the Prince made himself the first link between the composer and the English Court. The third acquaintance was the Duke of Manchester, then English ambassador at Venice. An ardent music-lover, actively interested in the production of Italian operas in England, he invited Handel to London. The invitation was declined, but another link, again aristocratic, was formed between Handel and England.

Early in 1708 Handel was again in Rome, enjoying the friendship and protection of two wealthy patrons of the arts, Cardinal Ottoboni and Prince Ruspoli. It was in the former's

* Newman Flower.

palace that Handel's oratorio 'La Resurrezione' and the allegorical cantata 'Il Trionfo del Tempo e del Disinganno' were performed. That summer he was in Naples, where he was lavishly entertained by Cardinal Grimani, the viceroy for the Court of Spain. Grimani was a Venetian, and his influence was consequently of great service during Handel's second and more triumphal visit to Venice. Grimani also wrote the libretto of the opera 'Agrippina' that was to win that triumph.

Invitation to Hanover

After his return to Rome early in 1709, Handel encountered Steffani, who was at the time Kapellmeister to the Elector of Hanover. Steffani invited Handel to become his successor, and Handel agreed. It is interesting to speculate whether Handel would have accepted this offer, the turning point of his career, had it come after instead of before his second visit to Venice. His life in Italy had been surrounded with every form of outward success. He had been received with deference into the highest circles of culture and nobility, and wealthy friends had eased his circumstances. But there was no prospect of stability in such an existence. Some conspicuously blank pages in the story of Handel's Italian years indicate that he was at times left to his own resources, for it is one of the characteristics of Handel's recorded life that when and where he was our only possible informant the information is apt to be lacking. No doubt these periods of independence taught him that a great reputation coupled with intermittent hospitality did not provide a means of livelihood. It was perhaps brought home to him, too, that the honours accorded to him as a distinguished stranger might be modified in the case of a Lutheran permanently domiciled in a Catholic country. As an alternative to this way of living, the prospect of a fixed post under a powerful prince must have offered solid advantages, even though it apparently meant giving up the ambition of an operatic career. Had the invitation to

Hanover come after the brilliant success of 'Agrippina' Handel might have preferred to take his chances in Italy, and a good deal of musical history, especially English musical history, would have been profoundly different.

Handel made his second journey from Rome to Venice some time in 1709, apparently as a stage in the direction of Hanover. Grimani's interest smoothed his entry, and on 26th December, the opening of the carnival season, 'Agrippina' was produced at the Teatro di San Giovanni amid scenes of extravagant enthusiasm. The opera was performed twenty-seven times, and 'Il Sassone' (the Saxon) became the talk of Venice. The next we hear of him is that he arrived in Hanover during the spring and was given the post of Kapellmeister to the Elector at an annual salary of 10,000 thalers.

First Visit to England

His installation was leisurely, for he soon obtained leave of absence in order to complete his period of educational wanderings. He paid a visit to his mother at Halle, spent some time at the Court of the Elector Palatine in Düsseldorf, and arrived in England late in 1710.

The descriptions that come to us of London in the early part of the eighteenth century do not present an amiable picture. Corruption pervaded high and low life. Morals were lax, and were to become still more so when George succeeded Anne. The town itself was unpleasant. The streets were badly kept, and violent robberies after nightfall were almost an accepted evil. The age was one that provoked the ablest literary men to satire. Hogarth was its artist, and seventeen years after Handel's arrival 'The Beggar's Opera' was its reflection on the stage.

The state of opera in London was not on the surface encouraging to the designs of a visiting composer except as a more or less barren field that he alone could invigorate. English opera, such as it was, had long been living a fitful existence. No operatic enterprise in England had ever been

free from financial stress—so early did fate show her hand
The factor that held out the greatest promise for Handel was
the recent vogue of Italian opera, at that time a novel sensation in the London theatre, and the chance of capturing the
new vogue while it was propitious. He set to work quickly.
Aaron Hill, who was producing Italian operas at the Queen's
Theatre, Haymarket, found him a librettist named Rossi,
and as fast as Rossi could write the lines Handel wrote the
music. In a fortnight 'Rinaldo' was composed. It was
performed on 24th February, 1711, and captured London as
'Agrippina' had captured Venice.

Handel was courted by society and began to make friends
and, at this early stage, enemies. The most conspicuous of
his ill-wishers was Addison, who had recently failed in an
operatic venture. Incensed by the success of 'Rinaldo,'
Addison attacked it bitterly, but unavailingly, in the *Spectator*.
Among the friends were two to whom we owe a good deal
of information. One was Sir John Hawkins, the historian;
the other was Mary Granville, then a child. Afterwards, as
Mrs. Pendarves and later still as Mrs. Delany, she was Handel's staunch friend through all his troubles, and her writings
throw many side-lights on Handel's existence. From Hawkins we hear of Handel as a visitor to the concerts of Thomas
Britton, the musical small-coal man. This famous eccentric,
a tradesman with a gift for music and a soul for artistic con-
verse, is credited with the beginnings of the public concert.
In a loft above his coal-selling establishment in Clerkenwell
he gave weekly concerts to which the public and later on
only subscribers were admitted. There the cultured aristocrats and leading musicians of the day used to forgather and
form a circle of the arts. Handel was frequently in this
company, playing on the harpsichord or the organ. Handel
also had the *entrée* to Burlington House, where sumptuous
musical entertainments were given by the young Duke of
Burlington. Thus, after a month or two in London, Handel
had established himself on the operatic stage, in the houses of
the nobility and among the celebrities of art. From these

conquests his duty to the Elector of Hanover called him away
in June, 1711.

Interim at Hanover

At Hanover he directed a small orchestra, taught music to
royal pupils, and wrote music appropriate to these tasks.
Of this dull interlude in Handel's life little remains but the
record of a gracious friendship. One of his pupils was
Princess Caroline of Anspach, whom he had probably met
on his visit to Berlin as a boy prodigy. They formed a
friendship that never weakened. Afterwards, as the wife
of George II, Caroline was unfailing in her goodwill and
support. Of Handel's relations with his Hanoverian master
there is nothing to tell. Whether as Elector or as King,
George seems to have taken but a lackadaisical interest in his
famous protégé. For the moment this was of advantage to
the composer, and when he sought leave of absence for an
undetermined period he obtained it. The only condition
laid down by the Elector was that Handel should return
within a reasonable time. The condition was not observed,
for this time London not only caught but held Handel.
This is the only occasion on which he failed to act according
to the highest scruples. To clear his character it is necessary
to ask which was more 'reasonable' destiny for a man of
Handel's genius—to play the part in the world for which
his nature fitted him, or to pass his days as a domestic musician
in a humdrum German Court. A likely explanation is that
Handel did not deliberately abandon his engagement, but
yielded to the momentum of his English affairs until it was
too late to hope for pardon.

The Londoner

Handel arrived in London during the autumn of 1712. By the
middle of January he had written two operas and seen them
produced at the Queen's Theatre. He had also experienced

the first of the many set-backs to which opera was prone in England. 'Il Pastor Fido' made little impression, but 'Teseo' was giving promise of success, when the manager of the season, one MacSwiney, decamped, leaving the bills and the singers unpaid. The season was, however, put on its feet again under the management of Heidegger, a man destined to play a large part in Handel's fortunes and misfortunes. Heidegger was a Swiss adventurer, of such self-confidence, address, and ugliness that he was admitted into certain ranks of society partly as a boon companion and partly as a butt. A man of talent and of business acumen, he ended by becoming rich at the expense of the English.

By 1713 Handel was living as the guest of Lord Burlington, or of the Dowager Countess, at Burlington House. He had, in fact, again taken possession of the English stronghold. His genius was everywhere acknowledged, and he lived in comfort. His ascendency over English musicians was absolute. When the Queen's birthday, or the Peace of Utrecht, called for a musical jubilation, none other than Handel was fitted to write the music. And there is no record of any complaint being uttered when Queen Anne awarded him a pension of £200 a year for life.

Handel's star never shone more brightly than during this early conquest of London, for though his name and fame were still to take deeper root, a lifetime of bitter struggle was to deaden the pride of his final victory. He was not yet thirty years old and could still survey his triumphs with the elation of youth.

The 'Water Music'

In 1714 the death of Queen Anne and the arrival of his possibly incensed employer in the capacity of King of England placed Handel in a predicament. There are two stories of how he got out of it. One is that the King was never really aggrieved by his Kapellmeister's truancy and was amiable to him from the beginning of the reign. The other is the

'Water Music' story. As this anecdote seems to be deeply
ingrained in English legend it may as well be told. The
King (runs the story) did not acknowledge Handel's existence. Lord Burlington and Baron Kielmansegg, the Master
of the King's Horse, therefore devised a scheme of reconciliation. On the occasion of a royal water-party on the Thames
they arranged that the King's barge should be followed by
another conveying Handel and a band of players. The
music was a suite of light pieces specially composed for the
occasion by Handel. The King liked the music and asked
the name of the composer. On being told that it was Handel
he immediately received the composer into his favour.
Whatever the true story of the reconciliation, it is certain
that the King gave Handel a pension of £200 a year for life
in addition to Queen Anne's pension, and that Handel went
with the King on a journey to Hanover in 1716. The evidence against the 'Water Music' story, discovered by Mr.
Newman Flower, lies in a document describing the scene in
some detail and attributing it to 1717, long after the King and
Handel had made friends.

At Canons

Meanwhile Handel had won a further operatic success with
'Amadigi,' which shared the popularity of 'Rinaldo.' By
1717 Handel found, however, that opera had gone out of
fashion and that French farces and ballets had taken its place.
He was ready therefore to accept an offer of employment
made to him the following year by the Duke of Chandos.
This wealthy parvenu (he had been Paymaster of the Forces)
had built a palace at Canons, near Edgware, among its
appurtenances being a private band and a private chapel with
a full musical establishment. Handel acted as master of the
Duke's music from 1718 to 1721, and for the adornment of
the services wrote the series of 'Chandos Anthems.' To this
period also belong the masque of 'Esther' and the serenata
'Acis and Galatea,' each of which has its importance in musical

history. 'Esther' is midway between opera and oratorio. It was written with a view to performance on a stage, but in its musical form it is perfectly adapted for performance on the concert platform. 'Acis' was also intended for dramatic uses and is equally suitable for the concert hall, as English musicians have faithfully observed for a century and a half. 'Esther' is now listed as the first English oratorio, and 'Acis' would pass as the first English choral cantata—'first' meaning the first to make a mark in the world.

Two of the best-known fictions connected with Handel's life are associated with this period. One is engraved on a tablet in Whitchurch Parish Church and declares that 'Handel was organist of this church from the year 1718 to 1721 and composed the oratorio of "Esther" on this organ.' Handel was never organist at this church, and he did not compose oratorios on organs. The other fiction is the 'Harmonious Blacksmith.' While Handel was engaged at Canons he spent much of his time in London, where he was giving lessons to the daughters of his friend Caroline, now Princess of Wales. Among the compositions of the time was a Suite of Pieces for the Harpsichord containing the famous Air and Variations, doubtless written for a royal pupil. The work was published without any adornment of title, and for a hundred years nobody thought of connecting the Air and its Variations with any blacksmith, anvil, or thunderstorm. The title was first attached to the work about 1820, when a publisher in Bath decorated it with the nickname of a blacksmith's apprentice, who was always whistling the Air. The legend of the Edgware blacksmith took its rise about 1835, to be followed in time by the discovery of an 'actual' anvil at Whitchurch and the erection of a memorial to the 'actual' blacksmith.

Handel and Opera

Before we bring Handel back to London a pause may be made for some brief remarks on the position of opera in his time. During the twenty years that followed the Chandos period Handel wrote over thirty operas; and in spite of the popularity that a number of them earned at the time the later world has consigned the whole collection to oblivion, apart from a small selection of favourite arias. We are accustomed to a high rate of mortality among the works of second-rate composers, but this complete extinction of a great composer's output in a specially favoured type of work does not seem reasonable. Various causes account for the phenomenon. The broadest is the fact that Handel was writing operas before the art of the opera had fully come into being. What he did was to take the existing form and fill it with better music. Immediately after his death the art began to treat him unkindly, for opera revolutionised itself. Gluck, Mozart and Weber gave the world an experience from which there could be no return to the stiff conventions of the Handelian manner, with its complacent succession of formal arias separated by stretches of dull recitative. From the later standpoint the operas of Handel were seen to be little other than stage concerts. And that is what they partly were in function. In the eighteenth century there were no public concerts of the now familiar type. The St. James's Halls and Queen's Halls of the time were the opera-houses, and people went to them for the kind of entertainment provided in modern times by the celebrity concert.

It has also to be considered how far Handel's temporary successes were won for him by celebrated singers. The leading singers of the time were male sopranos, the effect of whose voices we can only judge, now that the species has fallen into obscurity, by reports of the adulation they received at the time. Three of the most famous crossed the Handelian scene. Nicolini took part in 'Amadigi' and revivals of 'Rinaldo.' Senesino was engaged by Handel for the venture next to be described and re-appeared for season after season until he was displaced by the most famous of them all, Farinelli. The audiences that fawned on such creatures were conceivably even less responsive to music than the audiences that fawned upon the prima donnas and star tenors of a later age. It is easy to imagine that Handel was less assiduous in drawing the best out of himself for such a market than he was in tasks that called to him purely as an artist. This does not mean that Handel took less time over his operas than over his oratorios. The habit of writing works in a few weeks was as strong upon him in his late as in his early years. Nor does it mean that his operas are to be despised as music. The outstanding examples from 'Rinaldo' to 'Alcina' were the finest works of their type that then existed, and if Handel had written nothing else he would still have ranked as a distinguished composer.

The Royal Academy of Music

It was the dearth of opera that sent Handel to Canons, and it was a project to revive it that brought him back into the turmoil of the town. Two years having passed while the devotees of opera waited for the tide to turn, an influential group determined to bring the tide back for themselves. Their resolve came at a time when company-promoting was a popular hobby—it was just before the bursting of the South Sea Bubble. By this means it was proposed to collect the capital for a season of Italian opera. Lord Burlington and other peers were on the board, £50,000 was asked for and soon subscribed in £100 shares, and Handel was called in as director-in-chief of the music. Librettists were appointed. Heidegger was made stage-manager, Handel went abroad to engage singers, and everything was ultimately in order for a beginning in 1720. Thus was launched the most notorious operatic enterprise in history. The establishment that promoted it was called 'The Royal Academy of Music,' a translation of the official title of the Paris Opéra.

It was during this visit to the continent that Handel narrowly missed a meeting with Bach. According to Bach's biographer Forkel, Bach came to Halle from Anhalt-Cöthen, twenty miles away, to only find that Handel had

left on the previous day.   On returning to London Handel
took the house at 57 Lower Brook Street in which he lived
for the rest of his life.

After a winter of delays, the season opened in April, 1720.
It began quietly and did not wake up until Handel's 'Rada-
misto,' one of the finest of his operas, was produced at the
end of the month.   Early in the next season the Italian composer Bononcini, one of the musical directors of the Academy,
came out in a new capacity.   His 'Astarto,' with Senesino
in the cast, ran for thirty nights, and the famous rivalry
between Handel and Bononcini was soon splitting society
into factions.   A composite opera, 'Muzio Scevola,' to
which Mattei, Bononcini and Handel each contributed an
act, served only to fan the flames.   A cynical observer
summed up the affair in a well-known epigram:

> *Some say, compared to Bononcini,*
> *That Mynheer Handel's but a ninny;*
> *Others aver that he to Handel*
> *Is scarcely fit to hold a candle.*
> *Strange, all this difference should be*
> *Twixt Tweedledum and Tweedledee!'*

Hitherto the women singers had played an inconspicuous
part in the fortunes of Handel's operas.   But in the season of
1722–3 the genus *prima donna* suddenly appeared on the
scene in the person of Francesca Cuzzoni.   She was short,
ungainly and plain, but she had a voice that moved the town
to rapture.   Moreover she could sing Handel's songs as they
were meant to be sung.   In 'Ottone' (January 1723) she
helped Handel to win back his credit.   The combination of
composer and singer proved too strong for Bononcini, who
thenceforward receded from the position of rival.   With
both Senesino and Cuzzoni at his command, Handel went
from one success to another in 'Tamerlano' (October 1724),
'Rodelinda' (February 1725) and 'Scipio' (March 1726).
But meanwhile the Academy was not paying its way, its

affairs being conducted with an eye to display rather than to business. To provide a new sensation the management brought in a twin star to shine beside Cuzzoni. Faustina Bordoni, her only rival on the stage of Europe, became her rival on the stage of London. It can be imagined that the contention was far more spectacular than of two mere male composers. Society was again split, both by faction and by laughter. Handel induced the pair to take the boards together in 'Alessandro' (May 1726), carefully balancing their parts so that neither had precedence, and repeated the experiment in 'Admeto' (January 1727). The result was that disputes broke out in the theatre. In Bononcini's 'Astyanax' the riot in the auditorium set Cuzzoni and Faustina tearing each other's hair on the stage.

These scandals injured the credit of the Academy. The 'Beggar's Opera' applied the finishing touch. As the present world knows, that entertainment was not only a malicious but a witty and charming satire. It drew the town and helped to empty the Haymarket Theatre. In June 1728 the Academy came to an end, with nothing left of its £50,000.

Handel had meanwhile become an English subject. He was naturalised on 13th February, 1726, and at the same time appointed Composer to the Court and to the Chapel Royal. In the following year George I died. George II continued the pensions awarded by Anne and George I and added a further £200 as honorarium for music-lessons given to the Royal Princesses. When, for a moment, Handel cast off the toils of commercial opera and wrote the four 'Coronation Anthems' for George II, his genius shone at its brightest.

The Manager

The disastrous end of the Academy had so little daunted Handel that he decided to set up an operatic establishment of his own and to back it with all his savings, which then amounted to £10,000. He made a contract of partnership with Heidegger and planned a subscription season of fifty performances at the King's (formerly Queen's) Theatre. In the winter of 1728-9 he was abroad in search of singers. He visited old scenes in Italy and at Hamburg, and he paid his last visit to his mother at Halle. She was paralysed and blind, and died next year in her eightieth year. Handel's opera season opened inauspiciously in December 1729, one failure being succeeded by another. The operas, and the company, were admired well enough by those who retained a liking for serious entertainment. But the times were not propitious; society was partial to French farces and ballets, and to the numerous progeny of the 'Beggar's Opera.' The next season was more successful with 'Poro' (February 1731) as its centrepiece and Senesino as its chief ornament.

During this season there occurred an event of considerable importance in Handel's artistic development. The children of the Chapel Royal gave a private performance of the masque 'Esther' on Handel's birthday. The affair was a success and led to other performances, one of which was given without Handel's sanction by a rival *entrepreneur*. This roused the combatant in Handel. He added new numbers to 'Esther' and gave six performances at the King's Theatre. As a Biblical subject could not be acted on the stage, the music was presented in concert form. The Royal Family attended the first performance, and London did its best to follow suit. Thus was Handelian Oratorio born, and nobody seems to have been aware that a portent had been seen. When 'Acis' had been similarly transformed, and had proved as popular, some vision of the new possibilities had no doubt taken shape in the composer's mind. During the season of 1732-3 he experimented with the new idea. He composed the oratorio 'Deborah' and presented it during the opera season with raised prices. This act of prerogative marked the summit of Handel's fortunes as an independent manager. The season was to see the beginning of his downfall, for he had roused a powerful and unscrupulous enemy.

Operatic Warfare

It is not surprising that a character and a career such as Handel's should have provoked antagonism. He was a foreigner, of the race that Hanoverian rule had made detestable. He was a pervading presence, a busybody for ever intruding upon public affairs. He was an imperious and self-willed man. He had lately taken to ordering the amusements of the town in his own interests. And he belonged to the wrong party. At this time the King was openly at loggerheads with the Prince of Wales; and the Prince of Wales, being a likeable, spirited and popular young man, had on his side the brighter and more active members of society, among whom were people ready to vent their enmity to the King upon the King's musician. They formed a rival operatic company, put into it all the power of their influence and money, and set out to ruin Handel.

While this plot was being hatched, Handel turned aside for a while to attend to an invitation from Oxford. He was asked to give some performances of his works and to accept an honorary degree. Since he could not transport an opera he decided to give Oxford the benefit of the new and promising form of composition that had lately proved its usefulness. He composed the oratorio 'Athaliah' for the purpose and gave five performances of it during his stay at Oxford. For some reason or other he did not receive the honorary degree; it is believed that he refused it on being told that the fee would be £100. This was in July, 1733.

In December the Opera of the Nobility opened at a theatre in Lincoln's Inn Fields. Handel's opponents had bought over the popular Senesino and had secured a brilliant cast. The forces acting on Handel's side were the support of the royal party, his own indomitable spirit, and the fact that the music was his own. On the other side were ranged wealth, joy of battle, and low tactics. In July, 1734, when Handel's lease of the King's Theatre expired, he found that his enemies had slipped in and secured the renewal for themselves. He took the Lincoln's Inn Theatre for a month and then moved to the new theatre at Covent Garden. Meanwhile the opposition had secured the greatest prize of the day. When Farinelli appeared on the scene the worship of the male soprano rose to idolatry, and Handel found that his hitherto serviceable specimen, Carestini, was outshone. His hopes were buoyed by the success of 'Alcina' (April, 1735), and by the events of the following year, when, on the occasion of the royal marriage, he won the Prince of Wales to his side by a wedding anthem and a festive opera 'Atalanta.' During the spring of 1737 the operatic warfare was maintained vigorously, but in the summer it was brought to an end by the exhaustion of both parties. Handel had worn himself out. A physical and mental wreck, he went to Aix-la-Chapelle for a cure. His opera-house closed in June, his savings had gone, and he was a bankrupt. A few weeks later the Opera of the Nobility closed its doors.

Yet Handel had not finished with opera. When he returned to London, fully cured, in October, 1737, he had to take what means he could to satisfy his creditors. In company with Heidegger he gave a season at the King's Theatre in the early months of 1738. Apart from a lucrative benefit performance it was a failure. It is memorable only in that it included Handel's first and last comic opera, 'Serse.' One of the songs in this opera is 'Ombra mai fu,' which, under the title of 'Handel's Largo,' has never since ceased to go round the world.

In November, 1737, Queen Caroline, Handel's lifelong friend, died. He poured out his grief in the Funeral Anthem 'The ways of Zion do mourn.' It was characteristic of Handel that at this period of ill-fortune he occupied himself with a charitable task. He helped in the promotion of a Society for the Support of Decayed Musicians, and for the rest of his life he never failed in his efforts on behalf of the fund. The society afterwards became the Royal Society of Musicians.

Handel and Oratorio

As we have seen, there was no sharp division in time between the period of the operas and that of the oratorios. Nor was there a sharp conversion in the composer's mind from the one form to the other. Oratorio had on two occasions been his stand-by; it was as an alternative method of earning his own living, rather than as a new design for furthering the art of music, that he took it up for the summer of 1738 when the opera season had come to its normal end. In August and September he wrote the oratorio 'Saul'; in October he wrote 'Israel in Egypt.'

The libretto of 'Saul' appears to have been written by Charles Jennens, a conspicuous figure in Handel's later life. He was a rich and extravagant eccentric, possessed of some literary ability and of more conceit. He had built for himself a great mansion at Gopsall in Leicestershire and earned by his ostentation the nickname of Solyman the Magnificent. Handel was on several occasions his guest at Gopsall. The two appear to have got on well together in spite of the difference in their characters, and we owe a good deal to Jennens for the stimulus he gave to Handel in the composition of some of his greatest works.

In order to put the new works before the public Handel hired the King's Theatre for a series of concerts. 'Saul' had but a moderate success, 'Israel in Egypt' none at all. This is no matter for surprise. None of Handel's oratorios is more remote than 'Israel in Egypt' from the type of entertainment to which the public was then accustomed. A series of choruses that has but one parallel in the whole of musical literature was flung at an audience that had hitherto reckoned choral sounds among the side-issues of theatrical performance. It is small wonder that the work passed over their heads. Handel lost rather than gained ground by his first concert season. The 'War of Jenkins's Ear' helped to lower his receipts. In the autumn he opened the theatre at Lincoln's Inn Fields for a second season. The frost of that

winter froze the Thames and compelled him to shut his
theatre for two months. For the next season Handel turned
again to opera, wrote 'Imeneo' and 'Deidamia' and produced
them with an inferior company. The first had two performances (November, 1740) and the second three (January,
1741). Nothing was wanting to destroy his substances, his
hopes and his soul. His aristocratic enemies were not even
content to watch him sink. They hired men to tear down
his posters and to make trouble outside his theatre. He
retired to his own company and that of a few friends, among
them the faithful Mrs. Delany.

'The Messiah' and Dublin

Some time in the summer of 1741 Jennens gave Handel a
libretto that he had compiled from the scriptures. At least
he claimed to have compiled it. But Mr. Newman Flower
gives the credit to one Pooley, a clergyman who acted as
secretary to Jennens. The fact that the libretto is universally
admired and thus stands alone among the literary monuments
left by Jennens is an argument in Pooley's favour. Handel
set it to music between 22nd August and 14th September
and called it 'Messiah.' The English world, from the first
Press notice onwards, has preferred to call it 'The Messiah.'
The twenty-four days of its composition are to be counted
among the miracles of human achievement. Coming as
they did at the nadir of Handel's fortunes, they bring before
us, beyond the aid of words, the titanic force that lived in the
spirit and mind of this unconquerable man.

During that autumn Handel was invited by the Duke of
Devonshire, then Lord Lieutenant of Ireland, to give some
concerts in Dublin for the benefit of charity. The call to
charity was one to which Handel readily responded.
Coupled with the chance to shake himself free of London
and to test his fortunes in a new city, it re-awakened his
ardour. Early in November he departed for Ireland, taking
with him a company of singers. In Dublin he was his old

self, and Dublin made much of him. At Neal's Music Room, put at his disposal by the Charity Commission, he opened a series of concerts and continued it, with a never-failing audience, throughout the winter. He was greatly helped by two of his singers: Signora Avolio, a highly trained Italian, and the more naturally gifted Mrs. Cibber. This famous beauty, the most popular actress of the day, had come to Dublin out of friendship for Handel. Her singing was inexpert, but it had a living warmth of expression; and her talent was such as to enable her to undertake the soprano songs of Polly in the 'Beggar's Opera' and the contralto songs in 'The Messiah.'

This oratorio Handel withheld until the following spring. The first announcement appeared near the end of March. A public rehearsal was held on April 8th, and the first performance took place on April 13th. The choristers of St. Patrick's Cathedral and Christchurch supplied the chorus, and the solo singers were Signora Avolio, Mrs. Cibber, and male singers from the cathedral choirs. 'The Messiah' was received as a masterpiece. Handel did not, however, keep it in the repertory. From the first he treated it as a work apart, to be reserved in general for occasions of charity. The only other performance that he gave in Dublin was as late as 3rd June. In August he went to London, fully intending to return to Dublin during the following year.

The Second Failure

The events of 1741-5 were typical of the fluctuating drama of Handel's career. They set him upon his old pedestal, and they toppled him down again. The cause of his downfall was again to be nothing connected with art, but a feud against himself. The circumstances had, however, undergone a change. Instead of rivalry between one opera season and another there was to be rivalry between opera and concert. The opera season that Handel abandoned after the failure of 'Deidamia' was taken up by a group of titled people. As its fortunes ebbed the rising tide of success that momentarily attended Handel's oratorios was an offence. This time the composer was not caught up into artificial streams of faction. He himself was the enemy, and ranged against him were the forces of aristocratic privilege to whom it was intolerable that an upstart musician, a 'mere fiddler,' should presume to hold himself on their level, spring up again after he had been once ruined, pay every penny to his creditors (as Handel had done) and look the whole world in the face. They determined to ruin him again.

'Samson,' which Handel had nearly completed between composing 'The Messiah' and going to Dublin, was performed in February, 1743. It was well received and proved the mainstay of the season. The first performance of 'The Messiah' in London took place on 23rd March under certain difficulties. It was considered improper for the word 'Messiah' to appear on a playbill—for in the lack of concert halls the work had necessarily to be given in a theatre—and, whatever the name of the work, a number of people had scruples about attending a sacred performance in such a building. For some time it was entitled simply 'A Sacred Oratorio.' The reception was indifferent, even though King George brought the audience to its feet for the 'Hallelujah' chorus and set a fashion that has never lapsed. Streatfeild says that 'The Messiah' was performed only three times in 1743, not at all in 1744, twice in 1745, and then not until 1749. The cause of this apathy was no doubt that only a small section of the English people, and that the least serious-minded, had access to the work. It was only when 'The Messiah' entered into the consciousness of the population at large that it became a national monument. It was not published until 1767, and then at a guinea and a half.

Handel's position in the world was signalised late in 1743 when, as Composer of Music to the Chapel Royal, he wrote a 'Te Deum' and an anthem to celebrate the victory of Dettingen and all ranks joined in tribute to these splendid works. 'Semele,' the pleasant secular oratorio that we now

place beside 'Acis and Galatea,' should have given strength
to Handel's affairs (February 1744). But the opposition to
Handel had been growing and its methods were now relent-
less. Mrs. Delany says in one of her letters that there was *no*
disturbance at the first performance of 'Semele'—a revealing
remark. In 1744 the opera season promoted by the aristocratic party ended in failure. Handel hired the vacant King's
Theatre and in November 1744 opened a season designed to
consist of twenty-four concerts. That season was never
completed. By the only class of people who could have
ensured its continuance Handel was being discredited in
public and in private. 'Hercules' (January 1745) and
'Belshazzar' (March 1745), two masterpieces, were performed to smaller and smaller audiences. The season closed
prematurely. Handel was a second time bankrupt. (So it
is usually stated; but Barclay Squire has pointed out that his
name does not appear in the bankruptcy list.)* He went away
to rest his ailing body and his ailing mind. A few months
later he was making plans for concerts at Covent Garden.

Final Success

The Jacobite rising gave him an opening. The 'Occasional
Oratorio' appeared during the celebrations of the early
Jacobite defeats and aptly hit off the spirit of the times. It
was, however, 'Judas Maccabæus' that clinched the matter.
A work composed to martial themes and rising to a pæan of
victory, it caught the imagination of London before the
jubilation over Culloden and its aftermath had died down.
What is more, it caught a wider public than any that had
hitherto been drawn to opera or oratorio. Handel had formerly relied upon the system of subscription-tickets, a system
that more or less limited his audience to well-to-do-people.
From the time of 'Judas Maccabæus' he opened his concerts
to the general public and for the first time found an audience
whose hearts gave an echo to his music. Only in these last

* E. J. Dent.

D

years did Handel reach out to England, to meet with a hand-clasp destined not to falter until our times.

One factor in the success of 'Judas Maccabæus' was the support it won from the Jews. It has been said that Handel and his librettist of the time, the Rev. Thomas Morell, deliberately courted this market by returning again and again to the Old Testament for their subjects. A more cogent reason for doing so would have been the knowledge that the Old Testament was the foundation of English middle-class Christianity. Handel is more likely to have felt the pulse of his greater than of his smaller audience.

'Alexander Balus' (March, 1748) made little impression, nor was 'Susanna' (February, 1749) the success that it deserved to be; but 'Joshua' (March, 1748) and 'Solomon' (March, 1749) were well received. Meanwhile the earlier oratorios were gaining ground. Handel's fortunes were now set fair, and he was beyond the reach of his enemies. The celebrations of the Peace of Aix-la-Chapelle in 1749 served to bring him into the limelight of public affairs. A firework display in Green Park was a fiasco, but the mere rehearsal of Handel's 'Fireworks Music' in Vauxhall Gardens had drawn twelve thousand people and provided the sensation of the season.

The comparative failure of 'Theodora' (March, 1750) could not stir him, except to one of his *bons mots*. He said: 'The Jews will not come to it because it is a Christian story; and the ladies will not come because it is a virtuous one.'

Handel's charitable association with the Foundling Hospital dates from this period. After he had given a performance of the 'Fireworks Music' there in May, 1749, he was made a governor. He presented the Hospital with a new organ and opened it himself by playing at a performance of 'The Messiah' in May, 1750. This was the first of a series of annual performances that enriched the Hospital to the extent of eleven thousand pounds.*

* Newman Flower.

Blindness and Death

In January, 1751, after a visit to Germany, Handel began the composition of 'Jephtha.' On February 13th he wrote at the foot of a page: 'Prevented from proceeding on account of the weakness of the sight of my left eye.' His sight had been troubling him for some time, but never yet as seriously as this. His doctors told him the worst; he was suffering from *gutta serena*. Operations were of no avail. He became steadily worse, and by January, 1753, he was totally blind.

'Jephtha' was finished with difficulty during 1751. From this time Handel became more than ever dependent upon his secretary, copyist, and now amanuensis, John Christopher Smith, a man who owes his position in history to Handel's generosity. On one of his German tours the composer found an old University friend, Johann Christopher Schmidt, in reduced circumstances. He brought Schmidt to England and installed him as his assistant. Soon the whole Schmidt family came over, among them a boy of five. The boy was brought up by Handel, studied music, and succeeded his father as John Christopher Smith. After Handel's death it was from Smith that Mainwaring, Handel's first and least reliable biographer, attempted to draw some secrets—with little success, to judge by the results. Smith enters history as a diligent servant and leaves it as an uncommunicative informant.

With Smith's help Handel re-modelled his early Italian oratorio as 'The Triumph of Time and Truth,' and had it performed in March, 1757. During his last years he made additions and alterations to other oratorios. According to Burney his last composition was the chorus 'Sion now her head shall raise' in 'Judas Maccabæus.' Handel continued to play the harpsichord and organ and to direct the performances of his oratorios. His last public appearance was at the performance of 'The Messiah' on April 6th, 1759. The last illness came suddenly, and he died on the night of April 13th/14th. On 20th April they buried him in Westminster Abbey with the pomp due to a national hero.

Handel the Man

Though we are given scarcely a glimpse of Handel's inner being we can read the stronger lines of his character from his deeds. His strength of will must have been beyond normal measure. All his life he was moving mountains. A man so engaged does not summon patience at every check; it is to be expected, therefore, that many anecdotes of Handel picture him as hot-tempered. They are countered by anecdotes of good humour quickly restored. He had neither malice nor hatred. In a licentious age he lived decorously. To him, womanhood meant refined company. He had a reputation for uprightness in his business dealings, and we have seen that he was generous. He lived a life of Christian virtue without displaying any marked evidence of Christian piety. Of his general culture we got occasional hints. He had, for instance, a taste in pictures. All his life he preferred the company of cultured people to that of the frivolous.

In person he was imposing. His portraits show a stalwart and ample figure, suggestive of a certain heartiness at table, but well shaped and by no means corpulent. (An infamous cartoon representing Handel as a glutton was a deliberate exaggeration of a foible.) The features are not of the animated type. There is pride in their calmness, but no disdain. The good looks manifested in an early portrait are somewhat obscured by fullness of flesh in the later ones. Report speaks of his flashing eye and of the radiance of his smile.

Handel's 'Borrowings'

These have always been a vexation to Handel's admirers. Without apparently troubling himself with rights and wrongs Handel would appropriate a piece of music by somebody else and include it in a work of his own. If it is difficult to reconcile this practice with Handel's character as an honest man there is probably some factor missing in the inquiry.

In the first place, copyright was then but half established, either in morals or at law. In the second, Handel was not purely and simply creating works meant to stand as musical monuments; he was putting something together for immediate performance, normally by the ready process of composing it himself, or if this means failed in promptness, by throwing in anything that lay at hand—whether his own or another's work it did not greatly matter. To describe the process in these terms is not to vindicate it. The most convincing plea on Handel's behalf has been made by Professor Dent, who points out in his *Handel* that the borrowings tended to advance and recede with the composer's mental disorders. And in any case, Handel did not borrow the thoughts of others; he rescued them.

BIBLIOGRAPHY

CHRYSANDER, FRIEDRICH: *G. F. Handel.*★ 3 vols. (Leipzig, 1858–67.)

DENT, EDWARD J.: *Handel.* 2s. (Duckworth, 'Great Lives' Series. 1934.)

FLOWER, NEWMAN: *George Frideric Handel.* 21s. (Cassell, 1922.)

ROBINSON, PERCY: *Handel and his Orbit.* 5s. (Sherratt & Hughes, 1908.)

ROCKSTRO, W. S.: *The Life of George Frederick Handel.* O.P. (Macmillan, 1883.)

ROLLAND, ROMAIN: *Handel.* Translated by A. EAGLEFIELD HULL. 4s. 6d. (Kegan Paul, 'The Library of Music and Musicians,' 1916.)

SCHOELCHER, VICTOR: *The Life of Handel.* O.P. (Trübner, 1857.)

STREATFEILD, R. A.: *Handel.* (Methuen, 1909.)

★ Carries the biography only to 1740.

JOSEPH HAYDN

BORN 31 March 1732   DIED 31 May 1809

By Dyneley Hussey

Origins and Childhood

Although it is not susceptible of absolute proof, there is a
strong presumption that Joseph Haydn was of Slavonic
and not of German descent. He was born at Rohrau, a
village in Lower Austria near the Hungarian frontier. This
part of Austria, a rich alluvial plain, had been overrun many
centuries before by emigrants from what is now Jugoslavia
moving westwards under the pressure of Turkish invasions.
This is not the place in which to enter into the detailed
arguments which are set out by Sir Henry Hadow in the
essay mentioned in the Bibliography at the end of this Life
of Haydn. It must suffice to state that the names of both the
composer's parents have Slavonic affinities, that the village
in which he was born had also the alternative name of
Trstnik, and that Haydn's whole character seems essentially
not Teutonic.

But whether or no we accept his Croatian origin as proved
—and there are still some authorities who dispute it—there
is no question about the lowliness of Haydn's parentage.
He was the son of peasants. His father, Mathias Haydn, was
a master-wheelwright; his mother, Maria Anna Koller, had
been cook in a noble household. Franz Joseph was the second
of their twelve children, of whom only half survived infancy.
One of the younger brothers, Michael, also became a composer and was a colleague of the Mozarts in the archiepiscopal
household at Salzburg.

Mathias Haydn and his wife were both fond of music in

an untutored way, and it can hardly be doubted that the songs they sang, the father playing the accompaniments by ear on the harp, were the folk-melodies which their son was to civilise in his music. The child, too, soon began to sing, and proved to have a correct ear and a beautiful voice. It is recounted that, when some fiddler came to play in the village, the boy picked up two pieces of wood and imitated his movements. It is difficult to understand why this common enough piece of childish mimicry should have been thought astonishing. However, fortunately a school-master from Hainburg, a relative of the Haydns, saw this performance and detected in it signs of musical talent. He persuaded the parents to allow Sepperl, as the boy was familiarly called, to come to his school, though the mother was anxious that her son should be trained for the priesthood.

Johann Mathias Frankh, Haydn's first master, combined the duties of school-teacher and choirmaster at Hainburg. His teaching was strict and practical, and at the age of six Haydn was able to stand up 'like a man' and sing masses in the church choir and play a little on the clavier and on the violin. In his old age the composer expressed gratitude to Frankh 'for keeping me so hard at work, though I used to get more flogging than food,' and in another conversation he complained that his personal cleanliness, of which his parents had taught him to be careful, became neglected. 'I was,' he said, 'a regular little urchin.'

Another feat of his childhood was an impromptu performance on the drums in some outdoor festivity, which created a great impression. The incident must have had its comic side, for the drums, which are still preserved in the church at Hainburg, were strapped on the back of a hunch-backed boy in order that the diminutive player could beat them. His success as a drummer at this early age may well account for his later love of the instrument, and when he was in London half a century later for the performance of the 'Drum-roll' Symphony he displayed his skill to the admiration of Salomon's orchestra.

But for one of those occurrences which made Haydn's career singularly fortunate, the boy might have remained in Hainburg to become in due time a provincial choir-master and school-teacher. After he had spent two years there, in which time the young genius had probably absorbed all that Frankh could teach him, Georg Reutter, the organist of St. Stephen's Cathedral in Vienna, happened to visit the district with one eye open for likely recruits to his choir. He heard Haydn sing and carried him off to Vienna.

In Vienna

The good fortune of Haydn's removal to Vienna consisted not so much in a direct improvement in his education as in the fact that it brought him out of a backward provincial environment into a metropolis, where contacts could be made and genius could thrive on opportunity. In fact, the boy seems to have learnt at the choir-school little outside the ordinary curriculum of religious instruction, elementary Latin and, of course, singing, though he mentioned in after-life that he 'learned the clavier and violin from good masters.' Reutter, who was also Composer to the Imperial Court, was much too busy to instruct the children in the elements of harmony and counterpoint. Their schooling was left to two adult members of the choir, Adam Gegenbauer, who was also a violinist, and Ignaz Finsterbusch, who was more interested in his collection of pictures, Turkish armour and silver buttons. The boy was thrown upon his own resources, therefore, in order to satisfy his instinctive urge to write music. He got so little encouragement that, when Reutter found him one day engaged on the composition of a 12-part 'Salve Regina,' he laughed at his efforts and told him curtly to be content with two voices to begin with. Haydn's ardour was not to be damped by such snubs. 'I had the gift,' he was able to boast in later life, 'and by dint of hard work I got on.'

We must avoid giving the impression, however, that

young Haydn was a prig or what schoolboys elegantly term a 'swot.' He had his full measure of boyish fun and vigour. An anecdote related by Pohl indicates him as the leader in any mischief that was afoot. On the occasion of a visit of the choir to the Imperial Palace at Schönbrunn, the Empress Maria Theresa herself caught Joseph perched high on the scaffolding, which had not been removed from the newly completed building, in defiance of strict orders against such escapades. So the Empress instructed her Court Composer to give 'that blockhead with the fair hair' a good hiding. Haydn was delighted to be able to recall the incident to the Empress's memory when she was on a visit to Esterhaz.

That the boy was also well thought of by the authorities may be assumed from the fact that his brother Michael was invited to join the choir in 1745, five years after his own appointment. The brothers were together for three years and then Joseph's voice broke. Reutter suggested a means whereby the boy's voice might be preserved and strengthened. There was always a place for a good *castrato* in the Imperial choir or on the operatic stage. Fortunately Haydn's father, hearing of this barbarous proposal, stepped in and saved his son, and incidentally Music, from so great a calamity.

The authorities seem to have felt no responsibility for the future of the boy who had been the chief ornament of the choir. Whatever the immediate cause of his departure from St. Stephen's—there is the familiar story that he cut off another boy's pigtail—he left the school in November, 1749. Not yet seventeen years old, he found himself penniless and without resources in Vienna. But Vienna proved no stony-hearted stepmother and, with his customary good fortune, the youth fell in with a member of the choir at St. Michael's, named Spangler, who gave him lodging. Then he managed to find a few pupils and to borrow 150 florins with which he rented an attic and bought an old clavier and six sonatas by Emmanuel Bach. These he studied diligently, and upon them modelled the style of his early compositions. In 1751 or 1752, that is to say in his nineteenth year, he wrote his first Mass, which, according to Pohl, shows unmistakable evidence of undeveloped and unaided talent. Haydn's was not a precocious genius.

A casual acquaintanceship with an actor led to the composition of music for a farce, which was produced in Vienna and elsewhere. Another with Metastasio, the great Italian poet, who had lodgings in the same house, resulted in an introduction to Porpora, the most celebrated teacher of singing in Vienna. The old Neapolitan composer asked the youth to act as accompanist to his pupils. Haydn accepted for what he could pick up in the way of musical instruction, and became in effect Porpora's valet. When Porpora attended the Venetian Ambassador, whose mistress was among his pupils, at the watering-place of Mannersdorf, Haydn went with him. There he met, besides lesser celebrities, Gluck, who loftily advised the penniless youth to study in Italy, and Dittersdorf, for whom he conceived a profound regard.

In the meantime Haydn had been studying hard at theory, mastering the treatises of Fux and Matheson. He was, therefore, sufficiently equipped to make use of the next opportunity that fortune offered him. Karl von Fürnberg, a nobleman who was in the habit of inviting musicians to his country house at Weinzirl, heard of the young composer and engaged him as violinist. At Weinzirl, Haydn was able to test his practical ability as a composer of instrumental music. He wrote a number of divertimenti, serenades and so on, of which one was subsequently published without the wind parts as a string quartet (Op. 1, No. 5). Some of the works written at Weinzirl were for strings alone, and it was in this unobtrusive way, and not at the bidding of any intellectual urge to experiment in new forms, that Haydn came to write his first symphony and his first quartet.

Two Engagements and a Wedding

In the eighteenth century there was only one way in which an Austrian or German composer could make a living.

There were no public concerts, as we understand them, no adequate laws of copyright, no Performing Rights Society and, until the end of the century, few publications. Opera did not offer the same opportunities as it did in Italy. In Vienna the Opera was part of the Imperial establishment, and, even if the composers attached to the Court were sufficiently generous to admit a work by an outsider, they naturally supplied most of the operas performed. The only course open to the composer was to enter one of the Imperial, Royal or noble households as a member of the musical staff. Everyone with pretensions to aristocracy and with sufficient wealth had his own band and singers, just as—for the same reasons that they liked it and it brought them prestige— English gentry kept packs of hounds.

The composer's position was the same as that of any other domestic servant under the orders of the Chamberlain. If this seems to us an unworthy position for an artist, without independence or dignity, it must be remembered that at the time it was accepted as natural and, at least, it secured to the musician a livelihood and in most cases the opportunity to compose under something like ideal conditions. It is true that Mozart revolted against the indignities to which he was subjected in the household of the Archbishop of Salzburg, but his was, as we shall see elsewhere, a hard case.

The Kapellmeister in these establishments was charged not only with the composition of music for every sort of occasion —instrumental pieces to be played after dinner, operas to entertain his master's guests, cantatas to celebrate a birthday, Masses for the private chapel and, if any of the noble family fancied himself as a performer, compositions for his use—but also with the discipline, good behaviour and dress of the musicians. It goes without saying that the great bulk of the music turned out under these conditions was ephemeral, hastily written, performed once and then forgotten. It never occurred to any of these composers that he might be writing masterpieces which posterity would cherish. If the Kapellmeister was industrious and capable, he might aspire to one of the lucrative appointments at Court, though these often went to foreigners, or he might receive an invitation to London, where, if he were wise enough to leave the financial risks to an impresario, fortunes were to be made then as now.

Haydn was, perhaps, singularly lucky in his masters, but it cannot be too strongly emphasised that he earned his good luck. He pleased von Fürnberg sufficiently to secure from him a recommendation to Count Maximilian von Morzin, Chamberlain and Privy Councillor to the Emperor, who engaged him in 1759 as composer and director of music at a salary of 200 florins (about £20) a year with board and lodging. His appointment lasted only two years, for in 1761 the Count found it necessary to cut down his establishment and the musicians were dismissed. In the meantime, however, Haydn had come to the notice of Prince Anton Ester- hazy, one of the wealthiest nobles in the Empire, whose country estate was at Eisenstadt, thirty miles from Vienna. The Prince, whose Kapellmeister, Werner, was growing old, engaged Haydn as an assistant, and Haydn remained in the service of the Prince and his successors for the rest of his life.

During his employment by Count Morzin, Haydn took the one unfortunate step in his otherwise uniformly happy career. He married, and that in spite of the Count's objection to keeping married servants in his household. It is difficult to explain why he married Maria Anna Keller, the elder of the two daughters of a wig-maker in Vienna, to whom he gave music lessons. For everything we know about his character suggests that he had too much sturdy common sense to give way to pique. He had fallen in love with the younger sister, but she preferred the Church to a domestic life and entered a convent. So Haydn was weak enough to be persuaded by Keller to engage himself to Maria Anna, who was three years his senior, and whose shrewish temper can hardly have been unknown to him. The unhappy event took place on 26th November, 1760. Maria Haydn appreciated neither her husband nor his music, and, after some years of domestic misery, the couple parted for good. There were no children

of the marriage. Indeed, it is the sole touch of irony in
Haydn's story that he, who would have made an ideal father,
had no children but has, nevertheless, been pursued for more
than a century by a horde of symphonies and quartets
screaming 'Papa, Papa,' like the alleged children of Baron
Ochs in 'Der Rosenkavalier.'

Eisenstadt and Esterhaz

For the next thirty years the course of Haydn's life ran tran-
quilly. The only external events were the seasonal removals
of the household from the country estate in Hungary to the
town mansion in Vienna. The sojourns in Vienna became
less frequent when Prince Anton was succeeded by his
brother Nicolaus in the year after Haydn's appointment.
Not content with the castle at Eisenstadt, an enormous
building with seven towers and a moat, Prince Nicolaus
earned for himself the nickname of 'The Magnificent' by
building a palace modelled on Versailles, which he called
Esterhaz. The new buildings included an opera-house,
seating 400 spectators, and a marionette-theatre, besides the
Palace itself, which contained 126 rooms.

Prince Nicolaus was so pleased with his new home, which
was completed within four years, that he became less and
less inclined to move to Vienna for the winter season. This
proved a cause of grievance in the household, many of whom
had wives and families in the capital. Haydn himself had
little reason to grumble on that score, but he did complain at
times of his monotonous existence and also of the primitive
country fare provided in the servants' hall. At the same time
he realised the advantages of freedom from interruption and
isolation. 'My Prince,' he said, 'was always satisfied with
my works; I not only had the encouragement of constant
approval, but as conductor of an orchestra I could make experiments. . . . I was cut off from the world, there was no one
to confuse me, and I was forced to become *original*.'

The relations between Haydn and his master were, indeed,

most happy.   Prince Nicolaus was a genuine lover of music
and himself played the baryton (*a viola da gamba* with sympathetic strings), for which Haydn supplied him with a
repertoire.   He paid salaries that were, for the time, high,
Haydn receiving at first 400 florins yearly with subsequent
increases to 600 and then 782 (about £78).   When Werner
died in 1766, Haydn was advanced to the post of Kapellmeister, whose duties he had in fact been discharging.   Haydn,
on his part, knew his place without being sycophantic.
His good sense, his genial humour and his innate dignity
kept him on the best of terms both with his superiors and
with the musicians under his orders.   The well-known story
of the 'Farewell Symphony' is sufficient evidence of Haydn's
tact in dealing with a difficult situation.   It is said that the
musicians grew restive at the Prince's delay in going to Vienna.
So Haydn wrote a symphony in the *finale* of which the players,
one after another, ceased playing and, when their parts
ended, blew out the candles on their desks and left the room.
The Prince saw the point and took the hint.   Indeed he
would have been hard of heart, had he not been moved by
the melancholy beauty of Haydn's melody, which is so lovely
that, as Schumann said, it is difficult to regard the whole thing
as a joke.   Since, however, the story is well authenticated, it
is a warning against reading into the music of Haydn (and,
it may be added, of Mozart) the kind of profundity and
subjective emotion that became a part of the process of composition much later in the history of music.   Conscious
self-expression is one of the qualities that differentiate the
'Romantic' from the 'Classical' composer.

Of that other kind of experience, to which the word
romance is applied, there is singularly little in Haydn's life,
which may account for the lack of attention paid to it by
contemporary biographers.   Twenty years after his un-
romantic marriage, there began an attachment, scarcely more
romantic, since it seems to have been one-sided, to a young
singer at Esterhaz.   Luigia Polzelli was the wife of a violinist
who joined the Prince's orchestra in 1779.   She, like Haydn,

was unhappily married and the Kapellmeister fell in love with the girl, who was only nineteen and a mediocre artist capable only of taking minor parts. Signora Polzelli, one imagines from what occurred later, was more impressed by Haydn's position than attracted by a man nearly thirty years older than herself. For she quite shamelessly used his affection as a lever for extracting money and, when her husband died, induced him to sign a document promising that, if his wife died, he would marry her and settle a sum of money on her at his own death. When Maria Haydn did die in 1800 Signora Polzelli, who had put nothing in writing, was already married to an Italian singer. Haydn left her, none the less, a small annuity, though he revoked a legacy to her younger son, who had been his pupil and was popularly believed to be his child. Of this there is no evidence, and the cancellation of the legacy, which was only a small sum, affords a strong presumption that the belief had no foundation.

Another personal relation is more pleasant to contemplate. Indeed the friendship of Haydn and Mozart is one of the most charming episodes in musical history. They met face to face hardly at all, yet they conceived for one another an intimate affection based upon mutual respect. Nothing reveals the attractiveness of Haydn's character more clearly than his cordial admiration for the music of a man who was twenty-four years his junior—an admiration that took the sincerest form of learning from the younger man's example, so that his own genius only came to its full maturity after this most fruitful contact. There was no touch of condescension or flattery—for Haydn never took God's name in vain—in the older man's exclamation to Leopold Mozart after a performance of three of the quartets dedicated to him by Wolfgang: 'In the face of God and as an honest man, I tell you that your son is the greatest composer known to me either personally or by reputation.' Even more impressive is Haydn's modest refusal of a request from Prag for an opera, where 'Don Giovanni' had lately been produced, in which he says: 'I should run too many risks, for it would be difficult for anyone, no matter who, to equal the great Mozart. That is why I wish that all music-lovers, especially those with influence, could know the inimitable works of Mozart with a keen appreciation equal to my own. Then the nations would compete for the possession of such a treasure. . . . I am full of anger when I think that this unique genius is not yet attached to a royal or imperial Court.'

Foreign Contacts

In spite of his seclusion at Esterhaz, Haydn's fame had travelled abroad. The visits of foreign royalties and other personages in Austria, where at the age of thirty-three he was already regarded as a national hero, served to carry his reputation further afield. In 1781, for example, when the Grand Duke and Duchess Paul of Russia were in Vienna, Haydn wrote for them a set of strong quartets (known as the 'Russian Quartets'), for which he received the usual gold snuff-box set with diamonds. These quartets were printed by Artaria, who had become Haydn's publisher in the previous year, and their publication brought him an even more precious reward. For they stimulated Mozart to the composition of the quartets which he dedicated to Haydn. In the same year Haydn received an offer from William Forster, a violin-maker in London, for the publication of his works in England, and from Le Gros, the director of the *Concert Spirituel*, who had done little enough to help Mozart during his stay in Paris, a request for permission to print the 'Stabat Mater,' which had been given four performances with great success. It was not, however, for the *Concert Spirituel* but for the rival *Concerts de la Loge Olympique* that Haydn wrote the 'Paris' Symphonies several years later.

In 1785 Haydn was commissioned by the Chapter of Cadiz Cathedral to write an instrumental work suitable for performance on Good Friday. Haydn's fame had been carried to Spain by Boccherini, who was at this time in the entourage of one of the Spanish Princes. That his music was popular in intellectual circles as well as in society is proved by a reference in a poem by Iriarte, who also expresses his enthusiasm for Haydn in one of his letters, which is quoted by J. B. Trend in his article on Spain in Cobbett's *Cyclopedic Survey of Chamber Music*. For Cadiz he wrote 'The Seven Words of Our Saviour on the Cross,' which is described in the original edition as 'Seven Sonatas with an Introduction and at the end an Earthquake.' The work was subsequently arranged for string quartet and published in that form by Forster in London. The first number of *The Times* (1st January, 1788) contains an advertisement of it under the title of 'A set of Quartets expressive of the Passion of Our Saviour,' together with announcements of three of the 'Paris' Symphonies, two Symphonies by Mozart and works by sundry other composers. As Haydn heads the list, it may be assumed that his music was, thanks, perhaps, to the advocacy of Dr. Burney, already popular in London.

Burney had published some years before the account of his Continental journeys in search of material for his *General History of Music*. In the fourth volume, which appeared in 1789, he hails the composer as 'matchless and admirable Haydn! from whose productions I have received more pleasure late in my life, when tired of most music, than I ever received in the most ignorant and rapturous part of my youth, when everything was new, and the disposition to be pleased undiminished by satiety and criticism.' How many music-lovers have turned in their maturity, like Burney, to the music of Haydn and Mozart, when their appetites have grown jaded by the richer and grosser fare of more recent times!

When, therefore, Prince Nicolaus Esterhazy died on 28th September, 1790, Haydn's reputation was well established in the capitals of Northern Europe. In Italy he was less considered, for in Italy music meant opera; and, though he could turn out with perfect competence such dramatic entertainments as were required for the theatre at Esterhaz, Haydn had no particular gift for the stage nor any strong ambitions in that direction. But he had always wished to visit Italy and it seemed that now his wish might be fulfilled. For the death of his Prince, though a great personal loss, set him free. Prince Anton, the successor to the estates, dismissed all the musicians but those required for the church services. Under Prince Nicolaus's will Haydn received a pension of 1,000 florins a year, to which Prince Anton added another 400 florins, provided that he retained the title of Kapellmeister to the family. Haydn found himself, therefore, in possession of a comfortable sinecure and with plenty of vigour for the enjoyment of his ease and for the fulfilment of any lucrative commissions that might be offered him.

He was not long allowed to be idle. For he had hardly settled in Vienna, when he received a call from a man who announced dramatically that he had come to 'fetch him away.' Johann Peter Salomon was no Mephistopheles, however, but merely an impresario from London. He had produced symphonies by Haydn and Mozart at his Subscription Concerts in the Hanover Square Rooms in 1786 and in the following year he had sent Bland, a music-publisher, to negotiate with Haydn for a visit to London. Bland's mission was unsuccessful in its main purpose, though he returned to London with Haydn's 'best' quartet in exchange for his razor. Salomon was in Cologne when Prince Nicolaus died and he set off at once to induce Haydn to come to London. This time there was no reason for refusal and the terms were handsome—£300 for an opera for Gallini, the manager of the Haymarket Theatre, the same amount for six symphonies together with £200 for the copyright of the scores, and a further £200 for twenty other pieces. In addition Haydn was to receive the proceeds of a benefit concert with a guaranteed minimum of £200. Princely sums for a man whose salary had amounted to £78 a year.

All thoughts of Italy were dismissed and it appears that there had been more than thoughts. For, when he heard of Haydn's imminent departure for England, King Ferdinand of Naples, who was in Vienna, was highly incensed, and his expressions of anger suggest that Haydn was breaking a promise to go to Naples. Here it may be said that in his handling of financial matters and in his dealings with his numerous publishers, Haydn proved himself astute and capable. No one will blame him for putting up his prices as his popularity grew, but he laid himself open to a charge of sharp practice when, possibly by an oversight, he sold one piece to two English publishers. Forster, the aggrieved party, brought and won an action against the composer.

London

Haydn reached London on New Year's Day, 1791. He stayed at first with Bland until rooms were procured for him in Pulteney Street. He soon found himself a centre of interest in London Society. The Austrian Ambassador, then as later a patron of music, produced him as a national hero. The Neapolitan Minister, to whom King Ferdinand, relenting of his anger, gave Haydn a recommendation, together with the inevitable snuff-box, held a reception for him. Royalty invited him to St. James's, the City Fathers to the Guildhall, the various musical societies vied with one another to do him honour, and he was so much in request for dinner that he had to refuse himself to anyone without a title. Dr. Burney, who had welcomed him with a set of 'Verses on the Arrival of the Great Musician Haydn in London,' procured for him the honorary degree of Doctor of Music at Oxford University, and when he attended Commemoration in July to receive the degree, three concerts of his music were given, at one of which was played the last of his six 'Paris' Symphonies, thereafter known as the 'Oxford.'

The general public followed the lead of society and the connoisseurs, so that the concerts began in March in an atmosphere of hysterical enthusiasm such as is reserved nowadays for the personal appearance of a star from Hollywood or a record-breaking aviator. One 'fan' snatched his snuff-box (not one of the diamond-encrusted kind, but an everyday affair of no intrinsic value) as a souvenir; a hosier sent him six pairs of socks embroidered with motifs from his symphonies; painters, among them Hoppner, asked him to sit for them; and the Press, probably at Salomon's expense, proclaimed the brilliant success of the concerts.

There was trouble, however, about the opera. Owing to the unhappy relations existing between the King and the Prince of Wales, which affected every department of society, art and politics, Gallini, who had the Prince's support, was not allowed to produce opera at his theatre during the season at the Pantheon, which had the King's favour. Gallini thought to circumvent the difficulty by taking out a licence for music and dancing, under which he produced various vocal and instrumental works by Haydn. These entertainments failed to please and the opera, 'Orfeo ed Euridice,' was never completed, though paid for. Any disappointment Haydn may have felt was more than balanced by the success of the concerts. His 'benefit' realized £150 more than the guaranteed minimum.

Among the musical performances he attended in London was the Handel Commemoration of 1791 in Westminster Abbey, which provoked the remark: 'He is the master of us all!' He went also to St. Paul's for the meeting of the Charity Children, of which he wrote in his diary: 'I was more touched by this innocent and reverent music than by any I ever heard in my life.' He was touched too by the beauty of English women. There was a Mrs. Shaw ('the most beautiful woman I ever saw'), a Mrs. Hodges ('the loveliest ditto') and a Mrs. Schroeter, who so affected his heart grown susceptible in old age that, despite his engagement to the faithless Polzelli, he declared that, had he been free, he would have married her.

Haydn and Beethoven

Maria Anna Haydn was still very much alive and she wrote from Vienna to inform her husband that she had found a house in the Mariahilf suburb, which would suit her nicely, and asked for money to buy it. On his return to Vienna in the summer of 1792 Haydn bought the house for himself, added to it and lived there for the rest of his life. On the return journey he passed through Bonn, where a young musician named Beethoven was presented to him and showed the master a cantata 'which received the particular attention of Haydn who encouraged its author to continue his studies.' It is probable that at the same time the arrangement was made for Beethoven to go to Vienna as Haydn's pupil a few months later.

A great composer is not necessarily the best teacher for a young genius, and Haydn, at the age of sixty, fresh from his triumphs in London, was not, in spite of his own daring innovations, altogether sympathetic towards the headstrong and ardent revolutionary. Their personal relations seem to have been happy enough, at first, and entries in Beethoven's account-book show the pupil 'standing' his master a cup of coffee or chocolate. Beethoven, however, soon began to complain that Haydn's teaching had not 'the excellence which he supposed he had the right to expect' and that his master was too much preoccupied to give him adequate attention. He even declined to add the words 'Pupil of Haydn' to the title of his first work because, 'though he had received some instruction from him, he had never learnt anything from him.' Haydn was, however, too influential a person to be wantonly antagonised, and Beethoven's relations with him remained outwardly cordial during his period of instruction, which lasted until Haydn returned to London early in 1794. It is said that in later years Beethoven, on receiving a word of praise from Haydn on his 'Prometheus' ballet, retorted jestingly that it was no 'Creation' and that Haydn took offence. After Haydn's death, however, Beethoven repeatedly expressed his admiration for his old master and on his own death-bed he kept by him a picture of Haydn's birthplace, 'the cradle of so great a man!''

When Haydn was invited by Salomon to return to London

in 1794 on the same terms as before, he thought of taking Beethoven with him as a companion; but, whether because Beethoven was too proud to go or because Haydn thought that Johann Elssler, his faithful copyist, would be more useful to him, he finally decided to take the latter. Elssler, a native of Eisenstadt, had for many years acted as valet and secretary to Haydn, whom he served with a dog-like loyalty and with something like religious veneration. Haydn was growing old and needed such a companion to help him through the arduous work that faced him in London. For, lucrative though those engagements were, he had cause to complain of the amount of work involved, which left him 'tired out and exhausted.'

The second visit to London lasted from January, 1794, until August, 1795, during which period he wrote his last six Symphonies. His success, depending now less upon the novelty of his presence, was more profound than ever. The Court did him more honour than before and he was officially invited to make his home in England. But he was too much attached to Vienna and the Esterhazys to break away from them for ever and he returned home with a competence that assured him comfort for the rest of his days.

The Last Phase

During Haydn's absence in London Prince Anton Esterhazy died, and his son Prince Nicolaus, who inherited his grand-father's taste for music, proceeded to enlarge his musical establishment. He did not, however, call upon his old Kapellmeister to take any very active part in the reorganisa-tion, but Haydn resumed his summer visits to Eisenstadt. Haydn's salary was, nevertheless, increased by 300 florins in 1797 and again in 1806 by a further 600 florins, so that during his last years he was in receipt of 2,300 florins (about £230) from this source. For some years he continued to compose a new Mass for Princess Esterhazy's name-day. He also arranged the 'Seven Words' as a choral work, and it was given in this form at Eisenstadt in 1797.

In Vienna he wrote incidental music for a play produced by Schickaneder, part-author of Mozart's 'The Magic Flute,' as well as several religious works and the two sets of quartets, published as Op. 76 and Op. 77—the crowning glory of his chamber-music. That he was far from having worked out his mine of original inspiration is clear enough from his attack upon a form that he had hitherto not attempted— the full-scale oratorio. There can be little doubt that the deep impression made upon him by Handel's works in London inspired Haydn to emulation. The actual suggestion came from Salomon, who brought to his notice a libretto, based upon Milton's *Paradise Lost*, which had been written by Lidley for Handel shortly before his death. The libretto was re-modelled and translated into German by Freiherr van Swieten, and as 'The Creation' was produced privately in April, 1798 and in public at the National Theatre on Haydn's name-day, 19th March, 1799. The work was published in the following year and was quickly taken up everywhere. In London it was given at Covent Garden and at the King's Theatre in the spring of 1800 and it was included in the programmes of the Three Choir Festivals in that and the two succeeding years. 'The Creation' remained the chief rival of 'The Messiah' in popular favour, until Mendelssohn's 'Elijah' usurped its place.

At the instigation of van Swieten, who again wrote the libretto, Haydn followed up his success with another oratorio based upon Thomson's *The Seasons*. He undertook the work with reluctance, for he felt that his powers were beginning to fail. However, in spite of disagreements with his librettist about the suitability of some passages for musical setting, the work was quickly completed and was performed in 1801. This was Haydn's last big composition. The strain of writing it was too much for him and he often complained in his last years that 'The Seasons' gave him his finishing stroke. He wrote thereafter a few songs, including some arrangements of Scottish melodies, commissioned by an Edinburgh publisher. In December 1803 he ended his public career by conducting 'Seven Words' at a charity performance.

Haydn's creative strength was exhausted, but he lingered on for another six years, an old man full of honour, full of anecdotes. In 1797 he had been elected an honorary member of the Tonkünstler Societät in atonement for the pusillanimous treatment accorded to him by the Society twenty years before. But nothing touched him more deeply than the erection of a monument with his bust at his birthplace, soon after his final return from London. He was taken to see this monument and, entering the cottage where he was born, he knelt down and kissed the doorstep and pointed out to the company the place by the stove where his musical career had begun. So in Vienna, he delighted to tell his many visitors stories of his life and to show them the tokens—snuff-boxes, medals, even the packets of letters tied up with ribbon from ladies he had admired—accumulated during his long successful life. There was only one cloud upon his closing years. The French invaded his country, his love for which he had expressed in the finest of all National Anthems. In 1809 for the second time Vienna was bombarded and shots fell near Haydn's house. For an old invalid it was an alarming experience, but he called out to his servants: 'Children, have no fear; no harm can come to you while Haydn is by.' Even the enemy honoured him, and the last gleam of sunshine in his life was a visit from a French officer, who sang to him the air 'In native worth' from 'The Creation.' Deeply moved, he embraced his visitor. On 26th May he was carried to his pianoforte for the last time and solemnly played the Emperor's Hymn to his assembled friends. Five days later, early in the morning of 31st May, 1809, Haydn died.

Whatever veneer he may have acquired in his service with the aristocracy, Haydn remained throughout his life a simple peasant at heart. He had the peasant's unquestioning faith in the religion he had been taught as a child, which had

impelled him to put at the head of his scores, 'In Nomine
Domini,' and at the end 'Laus Deo.' His attitude towards
his masters had the same kind of simple devotion. It never
occurred to him that the existing order of society was anything but natural and right. For his art he had a profound
respect and, like the Englishman who dons his dinner-jacket
in the wilds, he never sat down to compose except in his best
suit and wig, while for an important work he wore the ring
given to him by the King of Prussia. In stature he was short
and ill-proportioned, and his face was, by ordinary standards,
ugly. But it must have been what the child called 'nice
ugly,' for no great composer had more natural charm, a
more genial temperament or a greater hold upon the affections
of all who knew him, than Joseph Haydn.

BIBLIOGRAPHY

BRENET, MICHEL: *Haydn*. Translated by C. LEONARD LEESE.
6s. (Oxford University Press, 1926.)
HADOW, W. H.: 'A Croatian Composer,' in *Collected Essays*. 15s.
(Oxford University Press, 1928.)
PARRY, C. H. H.: *Studies of the Great Composers*. 6s. (Oxford
University Press, 1887.)

WOLFGANG AMADEUS MOZART

BORN 27 January 1756   DIED 5 December 1791

By Dyneley Hussey

The Father of the Man

With the possible exception of Schubert, no composer has suffered more from the attentions of sentimental biographers than Mozart. Even in recent years books have appeared, representing the composer as a divinely inspired child who never grew up, a musical Peter Pan too dearly beloved by the gods. This view of Mozart would matter less, did it not encourage the damnable heresy that his music is so much innocent lollipoppery, the blameless confections of an infant mind endowed with extraordinary musical gifts. With the object of correcting this misconception, I propose to allot as little space as is consistent with a complete sketch to the often told story of his childhood, and to attempt a portrait, however summary, of the composer as a man.

The extraordinary musical gifts were there, indeed, and made themselves evident at an early age. At three the child was taking an interest in the music-lessons of his sister, four and a half years older than himself. Like any other child, he delighted in the sounds produced by hitting the keyboard with his fingers; but, unlike other children, he discriminated between concords and discords. His ear was so keen that he was soon able to detect a slight variation in the pitch of a violin. At four he began his musical studies in earnest, and at five he was composing little pieces which were copied by the proud father, not perhaps without correction, into his sister's exercise-book.

There is no accounting for genius, but at least Wolfgang Amadeus Mozart was no exception among composers in being the son of a musician. His father, Georg Leopold, was a violinist in the Archbishop's band at Salzburg, where Wolfgang was born. Georg Leopold's fame as a musician rested upon his treatise on violin-technique, published at Augsburg, actually in the year of his son's birth, rather than upon his competent mediocrity as a composer. The book became a standard work and was translated into several languages.

The better side of Leopold's nature is indicated in the general principles he laid down for his pupils. He demands of them unselfishness and patient application. Virtuosity for its own sake is frowned upon and the honest orchestral player is preferred to the brilliant soloist. Further, the musician must be a sound Christian (which may be translated into modern terms as a man of good morals apart from any orthodoxy in religious belief) and be possessed of a general acquaintance with the other arts, so that he may play with intelligence. Such enlightened principles of education are not unimportant qualifications for a tutor of young genius.

Leopold's character had another side. He was not free from the narrow prejudices of middle-class society in a provincial town. His letters reveal too often a man without humour, obstinate and too little charitable. His pusillanimity was displayed alike in harshness towards subordinates and sycophancy towards the great. Always ready to suspect the worst motives in others, he attributed to hostile intrigues any disappointment of his hopes. These faults arose in part out of his genuine love and concern for his family. He was ambitious for their success, transferring to them the hopes of great achievement which he had failed to realise in himself. In his attitude towards his son he was not unlike the Victorian father of convention, guiding his footsteps with tender care, but unwilling to allow them to make any independent explorations. Until long after he had reached manhood, Wolfgang was not allowed without a conflict to make any decisions on his own responsibility. The wonder is that the inevitable breach was not irreparable. Wolfgang's affectionate nature was able in the end to span it, and Leopold seems to have mellowed in his later years. His tenderness towards his children and his self-sacrifice in their interests, as he conceived them, are the redeeming features of an unlovable character.

As a music-teacher Leopold had little trouble with his son, who was obedient and docile. The difficulty, indeed, was to get the boy away from the keyboard, at which he played as other boys play with soldiers or railway-trains. Wolfgang's only other interest was in arithmetic, often the counterpart of musical talent, and he covered every available surface with his sums. At the age of thirteen we find him writing to his sister, Maria Anna, to ask for the rules of arithmetic and adding to his signature the high-flown title of 'Friend of the League of Numbers.'

If Wolfgang was in some things an abnormal child, many well authenticated anecdotes are evidence of a healthy mind. In spite of his acute sensitiveness, he was lively and full of not always innocent fun. In stature he was small, but he was not particularly delicate. Indeed, his physique must have been wiry to withstand the severe illness and nervous strain to which he was subjected in boyhood. He was deeply affectionate and craved in return expressions of the love he lavished upon those around him. Herein lay the source of that charm which never deserted him, even though hard circumstance was to sharpen his tongue and a blind faith in friends was to lead him into unjust prejudices. There was, indeed, in his nature a genuine core of sweetness upon which the sentimentalists have fashioned their icing-sugar statuettes.

A Prodigy on Tour

Leopold Mozart was quick to perceive that the precocious talents of his children—for 'Nannerl' also showed an astonishing facility—might be turned to account, and in 1762 the family started out on a 'celebrity tour' of Europe. The performances of the apple-cheeked boy, so pretty in his lilac coat, so lively in his intelligence and yet so unaffected in his manner, enchanted in turn the Courts of Vienna, Munich, Paris and London. The father's letters to his landlord, Lorenz Hagenauer, at Salzburg, are a series of exclamations, in which wonder is mingled with pride, at their triumphal progress, varied only by occasional attacks upon those who are supposed to have put in their way some obstacle to success. Now 'Wolferl' has astonished everyone by playing on an organ with pedals, without previous experience, and standing up; now he has fiddled their baggage through the Viennese customs; now he has told the Archduchess Marie-Antoinette that he will marry her, or been kissed by a Prussian Princess—though kisses will not pay hotel-bills—or has rebuked Mme de Pompadour for refusing a like salutation.

It is possible that Leopold's fond imagination exaggerated the musical and social success of his son, but there is plenty of independent evidence to show that wherever they appeared the children excited uncommon interest. In London, where they were announced as 'Miss Mozart of Eleven and Master Mozart of Seven years of age, Prodigies of Nature,' the boy was subjected to scientific tests by the Hon. Daines Barrington, the results of whose investigation proved that the boy's extraordinary powers were genuine enough. Some of his feats were, indeed, astonishing. At St. James's Palace he played pieces by J. C. Bach and Handel at sight, accompanied Queen Charlotte in an air and then improvised a beautiful melody upon the figured bass of a piece by Handel. His public appearances in London were an immense success, even though the attraction to the audience may have been sensational and sentimental rather than musical. Nevertheless it would be a mistake to suppose that at this early stage Wolfgang was already a creative genius. The pieces published in Paris and in London are no sure criterion of his ability as a composer, for they were certainly revised and corrected by the experienced hand of his father. The only authentic document of this period is a sketch-book, which shows that at the age of eight the boy was by no means a skilled musician. There are many mistakes and no signs of a real control over his material.

The Mozarts returned to Salzburg in November, 1766, after an absence of nearly four years in all. They were delayed by the illness, first of the father in England, then of Nannerl in Holland. But Leopold was, in any case, never too scrupulous about the performance of his duties to the Archbishop when they conflicted with the interests of his son's career. He has been blamed, not without justice, for his exploitation of the boy's talent at so early an age. To modern educationists the spectacle of a child being subjected to the fatigue of travelling under the conditions then existing, to the excitement of public appearances and to the adulation of sentimentalists, must indeed seem appalling. The marvel is that, whatever grave effects they may have had upon his physical strength, his temperament remained so remarkably unspoilt. Yet it is difficult to believe that his character was entirely unaffected by the attentions paid to him both by great personages and by the ordinary public. For the contrast between his easy successes as a child and the harsh difficulties that he encountered as a man may well have aroused in him the bitterness which embroiled him with authority.

From these early tours the Mozarts brought back no tangible gains, except the usual souvenirs presented by the great to musicians. Such money as they received—and Leopold was always grumbling at the smallness of their rewards— was swallowed up in expenses. But travelling in foreign lands and contacts with musicians like J. C. Bach undoubtedly had a great effect upon the mind of even so young a boy and developed his precocious talent. He was soon kept busy on his return to Salzburg by commissions from the Archbishop and others who wished to make use of the now celebrated young genius. It was recorded that the Archbishop, sceptical of his powers, had him shut up by himself while he composed a cantata. In the meantime he was set to study composition in earnest, his chief models being P. E. Bach, Hasse and Handel.

In the autumn of 1767, a year after their return to Salzburg, the family again visited Vienna, where the wedding-festivities of the Archduchess Maria Josepha held out prospects of a profitable season. These hopes were not realised, for an epidemic of smallpox carried off the bride among its victims, and the Mozart children contracted the disease at Olmütz, whither they had retired to avoid it. With singular generosity, the Dean of Olmütz took them into his house, and though Wolfgang was seriously ill both he and his sister recovered. The boy had some years before had a severe attack of scarlet fever, and it may well be that these illnesses caused that lack of lustre in his eyes so noticeable in later life.

The Mozarts returned to Vienna in January, 1768, and, with the approval of the Emperor Joseph, who had succeeded to the throne four years before, Leopold obtained for his son a commission to write an opera. Gluck looked with favour upon the project, but Afflisio, the manager of the Opera, was not convinced of the wisdom of producing a work by a boy of twelve, and the project fell through. As a result of a petition from the aggrieved Leopold, the Emperor ordered 100 ducats (about £45) to be paid by way of compensation. The young composer was further consoled by the performance at the house of Dr. Anton Mesmer of 'Bastien und Bastienne,' a little piece of considerable charm though of no outstanding genius, and the earliest of Mozart's dramatic works to retain its place in the modern theatre.

Italy

In the eighteenth century, music meant, first and foremost, Italian opera, and it was to Italy that composers looked for their education, just as, a hundred years later, students flocked to Leipzig and Dresden in order to study German symphony. Handel served his apprenticeship in Italy; Bach based much of his music upon Italian models. It was natural that Leopold Mozart should wish his son to drink at the living source of current musical practice, and to exhibit his powers in the capital of the artistic world. He had intended to proceed to Italy from Vienna before 'Wolfgangerl should have reached the age and stature which would deprive his accomplishments of all that was marvellous.' He saw in the boy nothing more than a precocious talent, which must be exploited to the full, before he grew to manhood and settled down as a respectable musician like his father.

Leopold had, however, to return to Salzburg at the beginning of 1769, and was unable to obtain further leave of absence until the end of that year. In the meantime Wolfgang had been appointed Concert-master. The post carried at first no salary, and it is not known when he began to receive the £14 a year, which was his stipend eight years later. The shades of the prison-house were beginning to close about the growing boy, who had basked in the sunshine of royal smiles and popular admiration.

At this time begin those letters of Mozart, which are the most revealing documents that any composer has left for historians. The boy's character is plainly to be seen even in these early letters from Italy, most of them no more than postscripts to Leopold's correspondence with his wife and daughter, who remained on this occasion at Salzburg. Already there are signs of that keen dramatic sense, of that ability to draw a character in a phrase, which was to place him in the front rank of operatic composers. There is an immense sense of fun, which was later to develop into a less pleasant form of jesting, but, where music is concerned, there is already a complete seriousness. Even to the boy of thirteen, music was the central fact of existence, a matter to be treated with the same seriousness and reverence as religion. Other subjects were matters for puns, jingles and rigmaroles in three or four languages. It is as if the boy were cutting his literary teeth upon the hard bones of words, and his mature letters are, not least in their idiosyncrasy of style, very

remarkable literary efforts and unique among the records of
musicians. His achievement is the more extraordinary in
that his education seems to have been rudimentary in everything except music. He displayed no particular interest in
literature. His taste lay in the direction of fantastic tales.
The Arabian Nights, presented to him by an Italian admirer,
particularly delighted him. The works of Metastasio, the
great Italian poet and librettist, appealed to him rather as a
young opera-composer learning his trade than as a student
of poetry. Here it may be added that there is not a single
reference in his letters to the masterpieces of painting, which
he can hardly have failed to see during his travels, nor to the
natural beauties of the Italian scene. Music was what he
had come to study, and it engaged the whole of his mind,
provoking comments that are astonishingly acute as well as
wholly serious.

This Italian visit was completely successful. In Milan he
secured a commission to write an *opera seria*. In Bologna he
made a deep impression alike upon Padre Martini, the *doyen*
of Italian musicians, and upon Farinelli, the great singer,
who was living there in retirement. In Rome he performed
the astonishing feat of writing out from memory after a
single hearing the famous 'Miserere' by Allegri, the exclusive
property of the Papal Choir which no one was allowed to
copy under penalty of excommunication. The Pope, however, bestowed upon the boy the Order of the Golden Spur
and he was able to add to the collection of whimsical signa-
tures at the end of his letters, 'Chevalier de Mozart.' At
Naples, where he was entertained by Sir William Hamilton,
the English Ambassador, he was suspected by the superstitious
Neapolitans of black magic and had to prove to them that
he could play as well without as with the ring which was
supposed to be the source of his extraordinary powers.

On his way back to Milan for the production of his opera,
he was admitted after a severe examination to membership
of the Philharmonic Society of Bologna, at the unprecedented
age of fourteen. In spite of the misgivings aroused by the

E

age of the composer, the opera, 'Mithridates, King of Pontus,' pleased both the singers and the public, and the 'Cavaliere Filarmonico' was hailed with cries of 'Viva il Maestrino!' 'Mitridate' was given twenty performances during the season, after its production in December, 1770. The membership of the Philharmonic Society of Verona was added to Mozart's honours and he received a commission to compose a dramatic serenade for the approaching marriage of the Archduke Ferdinand. Here was the climax of his infant fame, and amid this blaze of glory the boy passed into manhood.

To the fond Leopold it seemed that his son was made for life. He could not see that in composing 'Mitridate' the boy had shown nothing more, though that was astonishing enough, than a facility for pouring music into an existing mould. There was still no individual creative imagination in his music. One of Burney's correspondents, writing from Salzburg a few months later, summed up the true position, as it appeared to an impartial witness: 'If I may judge of the music which I have heard of his composition, in the orchestra, he is one further instance of the early fruit being more extraordinary than excellent.' A second shrewd observer, the composer Hasse, had other fears: 'Young Mozart,' he wrote, 'is certainly a prodigy for his age and I am extremely fond of him. The father . . . adores his son overmuch and does all he can to spoil him; but I have so good an opinion of the innate goodness of the boy that I hope that, despite his father's adulation, he will not allow himself to be spoilt, but will turn out an honourable man.'

Salzburg

The Archiepiscopal Court at Salzburg, in which he occupied so insignificant a place, must have appeared doubly dreary to the boy after the freedom and the excitements of Italy. Salzburg was a city without any important industry, in which everyone from the impoverished nobles downwards lived on pickings from the Court, and the Prince-Archbishop was no longer the wealthy and powerful figure of a hundred years before. The people spoke a clipped dialect of German with narrowed vowels and dropped consonants, which affords parallels with certain American corruptions of English. Salzburg becomes Soisburg as girl becomes 'goil' or work 'woik.' Besides this dialect, which Mozart often uses for fun in his letters, the Soisburgers had their own brand of humour, which was embodied in the figure of Hanswurst, a character in the German marionette plays. This personage, whose name may be rendered as 'Jack-Pudding,' made jokes in 'poor' taste or worse. We shall have occasion to see that in some respects Mozart was a true member of the Salzburg middle class, and that he was not unjust to himself in signing some of his letters with the name of Hanswurst.

The Archbishop, under whose rule he was born, was Sigismund Schrattenbach, an old-fashioned disciplinarian, who seems to have allowed his musical establishment to deteriorate in quality, if not in numbers. There were nearly 100 musicians at his Court, but, according to Burney, they were 'more remarkable for coarseness and noise than for delicacy and high-finishing.' It is small wonder that the boy was deeply impressed when he heard the famous Mannheim orchestra at Schwetzingen on the way to Paris and London. Sigismund died in 1771 on the day of Mozart's return from a second visit to Milan for the reproduction of 'Lucio Silla,' an opera which failed to repeat the success of 'Mitridate,' and Hieronymus von Colloredo, Bishop of Gurk, was translated to the Archbishopric.

Hieronymus has been represented as the evil genius of Mozart, and, in the light of subsequent history, it is easy to accuse him of harshness and lack of imagination. He was, in fact, a man of considerable distinction in the Church and State, independent, enlightened and tolerant. He was interested in music to the extent of reforming his establishment and improving its standards and, if he preferred Italian music to German, that was not unnatural in view of his own origin and the fashions of the time. He was not inclined, therefore, to further the ambitions of his touchy German Vice-Kapellmeister, Leopold Mozart, and infuriated him by importing an Italian to take command of his musicians when the post fell vacant.

The failure of 'Lucio Silla' was due to several causes. It had a poor libretto; its impressionable composer, who readily adapted himself to his musical environment, had been out of touch with Italy for nearly two years; and he had passed the age at which everything he did was certain to provoke the astonishment and win the sympathy of his audience. It was an important turning-point in Mozart's career, for it ruled out the possibility of his developing into an Italian composer, like Handel and Hasse. A visit to Vienna, whither the Archbishop went in 1773, renewed Wolfgang's contact with German music, this time in the compositions, if not the person, of Joseph Haydn. Haydn's was the most powerful single influence upon Mozart's development as a composer, and from this time he began to speak of the older man as his 'master.' Their personal relations have been described in the Life of Haydn in this volume, to which the reader is referred. The visit to Vienna was, therefore, fruitful, though it failed of its immediate object, which was to obtain for Wolfgang a post in the capital.

A year later, in December, 1774, Mozart again left Salzburg for a visit to Munich, whence he had received a commission to write a comic opera. 'La Finta Giardiniera,' which was produced in the following January, had a great success and its composer was once more spoken of as a 'wonderful genius.' Yet he received no tangible reward in the way of an appointment. On his return to Salzburg, Leopold set him to work harder than ever at violin-playing. His father (no mean judge) was of the opinion that, if he would do himself justice, he would be 'the first violinist in Europe.' The results of his application are embodied in the five violin concertos, all written at this time. But although he worked at the instrument to please his father, Wolfgang

had no great love for it, and turned his attention to the newly
invented pianoforte as soon as he cut his apron-strings.

The year 1776 was busily spent in composition. Pianoforte concertos, organ sonatas, Masses and divertimenti,
including the well-known 'Haffner Serenade,' composed for
the wedding of the Burgomaster's daughter, came tumbling
from Mozart's prolific pen. But discontent with his position
was growing. He was disgusted with the lack of any real
interest in art, with the company he had to keep at the
Archbishop's table, and above all with the attitude of the
Archbishop himself, who would neither recognise his merits
nor let him seek fame elsewhere. For when Leopold, who
was becoming anxious at the growing strain in the relations
between his son and his master, applied for leave to go on
yet another tour, it was refused. Wolfgang called the
Archbishop's bluff by applying for his discharge; and that
dignitary, who had no wish to lose him, retorted with an ill
grace that both father and son might seek their fortunes
where they pleased—which in less archiepiscopal language
meant that they were free to go to the devil. Leopold was,
in the event, not allowed to leave Salzburg, and with great
reluctance he despatched his son in the company of his wife
and with more paternal admonitions than those that sped
Laertes upon his travels.

Aloysia and the Bäsle

Paris was the ultimate objective of this tour. Leopold hoped,
on the strength of Wolfgang's success in the French capital
as a child, that all doors would be open to the young man of
one-and-twenty, and that some lucrative post at Court would
quickly be offered to him. Not that the travellers were to
miss any opportunities that might offer themselves on the
way to Paris. So mother and son, setting off in their new
carriage, bought at great self-sacrifice, first visited Munich,
where on 30th September, 1777, the young composer humbly
offered his services to the Elector of Bavaria, only to receive

the reply, 'Yes, yes, my dear child, but there is no vacancy, I am sorry to say. If only there were a vacancy!'

At Augsburg, Mozart found more congenial company. He divided his time between Andreas Stein, whose new pianofortes aroused his keen interest, and his cousin, Maria Anna Thekla Mozart, of whom he writes, 'We suit one another very well, for like me she is rather naughty; we laugh at everybody and have great fun!' This remarkably plain young woman, the daughter of Leopold's brother, brought out the Hanswurst in Wolfgang and the fun they had seems to have consisted mainly of jokes connected with that humble part of the human body upon which men sit. That Wolfgang was really in love with his 'Bäsle' (cousin), as he always calls the girl, is psychologically improbable. He certainly flirted with her, as he had flirted with any girl who came within his reach for some years past. To his father he writes about the Bäsle with a mocking rapture, which rules out of question a serious entanglement, though not a genuine affection. So much has been made of the indecency of Mozart's conversations and correspondence with his cousin, that it is as well to state frankly that, for the most part, they consisted of nothing worse than, for example, singing in a part-song, in place of the proper words, 'Padre Emilian, you booby, you may kiss my a——!' If this seems impolite language to use in the presence of a young girl, the difference of eighteenth-century manners from those of the recent past must be taken into account. Such expressions—and I can find nothing worse in the published letters*—hardly argue a base morality in the young man and their importance has

---

* It is true, however, that Schiedermair has, with more prudery than befits a scientific editor, omitted one or two passages from his edition of the letters. These blanks, occupying not more than half-a-dozen lines in all, presumably contained sexual indecencies of some kind. But I am not prepared to admit that, in the face of the evidence to the contrary, these adolescent indelicacies are proof of Mozart's immorality.—D. H.

been grossly exaggerated by writers who have reacted against the view of Mozart as an innocent child. Mozart was neither innocent nor a profligate. He was, as he says in one of the most dignified defences of his conduct against his father's misconstruction of his actions, a man like other men, and one in whom 'perhaps nature speaks more strongly than in many big and vigorous louts.' In an age of loose morals Mozart stands out, on the evidence of his letters and his actions, as a man, not always impeccable, but controlled by that idealism in his relations with women that is one of the marks of a noble character. Whatever the shortcomings of Leopold's education of his son in other practical matters, he must at least be credited with fostering, in his somewhat narrow and puritanical way, this side of Wolfgang's nature.

From Augsburg the travellers went to Mannheim, the seat of Prince Karl Theodor, one of those German princes who sought to emulate the glories and the vices of Versailles. The vices have passed away, but the glories remain in one of the finest pieces of town-planning in the world, whose severity of ordered outline is made warm and beautiful by the rosy stone of which the houses are built. Here Wolfgang fell seriously in love. Among the musicians in the town was Fridolin Weber, a copyist, who had four daughters, of whom the eldest, Josepha, was the possessor of a remarkable voice and has her place in musical history as the creator of the part of the Queen of the Night in 'The Magic Flute.' The second daughter, Aloysia, was also a singer, and Wolfgang soon began to write of her to his father with a discreet enthusiasm, while the lively correspondence with the Bäsle at Augsburg temporarily ceased. Finally the young man proposed that he should abandon his visit to Paris and accompany the Weber family on a tour in Italy. Leopold received this hare-brained project 'with amazement and horror' and ordered his son to be off to Paris. For the first time Wolfgang showed signs of revolt against his father's oppressive guardianship. He is no longer a child, he writes, and, though his love and respect are undiminished, he will not tolerate accusations about his conduct with Aloysia. 'There are some people,' he says scornfully, 'who think it impossible to love a girl without evil designs and this pretty word *mistress* is indeed a fine one !'

Leopold was adamant and Wolfgang eventually departed for Paris in the middle of March, 1778. The visit was completely unfruitful. Melchior Grimm, who had helped the infant prodigies fifteen years before, was less interested in a young man without the social attractions of a resounding success and was frankly bored by Leopold's tedious screeds about his son's marvellous gifts. Grimm was a lion-hunter, to whom genius was synonymous with success. Le Gros, the director of the 'Concert Spirituel,' was no more helpful. Projects for an opera came to nothing and the only work that Mozart composed for the Parisian stage was the ballet, 'Les Petits Riens.' He was, indeed, offered the post of organist at Versailles with a salary of 2,000 livres (about £90), which Leopold urged him to accept. But Mozart rightly felt that Versailles was a backwater and Paris, pre-occupied with the rivalry of Gluck and Piccinni, no place for an unknown German composer. Possibly, too, he was influenced by thoughts of the separation from Aloysia, which acceptance would involve. While he was still undecided, his mother fell ill and on 3rd July she died.

For the first time in his life, Mozart was alone in the world. He remained in Paris until the end of September, seemingly stunned and incapable of action. His father now urged him to return to Salzburg, where there were prospects of his advancement owing to the deaths of the organist and the Kapellmeister. Wolfgang was appointed on his return to the former of these posts with a salary of about £40, but the latter was given, as I have related, to an Italian. Salzburg held no attractions for the young man and he made no haste to reach home. His first objective was, not unnaturally, Mannheim, but the Court and with it the Weber family had moved to Munich. At Mannheim he received peremptory orders to return at once. So he left—for Munich. A

sorry figure in his mourning clothes, he presented himself to
Aloysia.   But she had become in the meantime a successful
singer and thought she could do better for herself than link
her fortunes with a composer of little outward favour and
less worldly success.   Wolfgang, the story goes, sat down at
the pianoforte and sang, with a mixture of bitterness and
humour, to the melody of 'Ich lass das Mädel gern, dass mich
nicht will,' words in the vein of his letters to the Bäsle.
That young person, by the way, had been cajoled into coming
to Munich 'to play a great *rôle*,' which was apparently to be
bridesmaid at her fickle cousin's wedding.   Aloysia's idea of
bettering herself was to marry a travelling actor named
Lange, whose sole distinction is that some years later he
painted the best portrait of Mozart.

In spite of Leopold's entreaties and commands Wolfgang
could not tear himself away from Munich.   He found con-
solation in the company of his spritely cousin, with whom he
concocted joint epistles to Salzburg full of jibes and puns.
A blot is turned into a portrait 'of my cousin writing in her
shirt-sleeves' and the word 'cousin' before her signature is
altered to 'cochon.'   Such fooling infuriated Leopold, and
he commanded Wolfgang peremptorily to return home.   At
last in the middle of January, 1779, Wolfgang obeyed, but
he took his 'dear little Bäsle' with him.

Constanze

It was a sad and disillusioned young man who took his
place at the Archbishop's table between Ceccarelli, the male
soprano, and the disreputable violinist, Brunetti.   Their
company and the whole atmosphere of Salzburg were more
than ever repugnant to his sensitive nature.   He settled down
to his duties as organist, composing music for the Cathedral
as well as symphonies and divertimenti.   He also tried his
hand at a German opera to a libretto by his friend Schachtner,
the horn-player.   This was interrupted by a commission to
write an *opera seria* for the Munich Carnival of 1781.   He was

given a long-winded and ineffective libretto concocted, in poor imitation of Metastasio, by the Archbishop's chaplain. The theme was the story of the return from Troy of Ido-meneo, King of Crete, who made the same rash vow as Jephthah.

Mozart's letters from Munich concerning his troubles with Raaf, the elderly tenor, who was only too willing to give the composer the benefit of his experience, and the juvenile dal Prato ('*mio molto amato castrato dal Prato*'), a boy of sixteen who had no experience at all, make amusing read-ing. They contain, too, the only considerable record of Mozart's views upon opera. Mozart was never a conscious theorist, and rarely expressed his ideas about music as an art. His grasp of the principles of operatic, as of symphonic, composition was intuitive rather than intellectual. It is fortunate for us, therefore, that circumstances compelled him to put down on paper his reasons for altering the libretto of 'Idomeneo,' so that Leopold might pacify the author. It is a pity that the crucial passages are omitted from the latest English translation of the *Letters*, but the reader who is interested will find them summarised in the chapter on 'Idomeneo' in my book on Mozart.

'Idomeneo,' a classical *opera seria* in the manner of Gluck, had a momentary success, but its production led to no advancement for the composer. Wolfgang was summoned from Munich to join the Archbishop at Vienna, whither he had moved with part of his musical staff, Leopold being left behind at Salzburg. Wolfgang's letters to his father reveal his ever growing discontent with his position. Sarcastically he congratulates himself upon having the honour to sit above the cooks at table, and grumbles at the allowance of three ducats paid when no meal was provided. 'The Arch-bishop is glad enough to get credit from his people; he takes their services and does not pay for them.'

The storm was brewing and in vain Leopold counselled his son to have patience. With incredible meanness the Archbishop at first refused to allow his organist to appear at a charity concert, and, although he had to yield on this point, Wolfgang was not permitted to give a concert for his own benefit. When to these injuries there were added insults, Mozart decided that, despite his father's entreaties, he would endure such indignities no longer. The Archbishop, who was unpopular with the Emperor and the nobility, took offence at not receiving an invitation to the summer residence of the Court at Laxenburg, and decided to return at once to Salzburg. Mozart was told to clear out of the house at short notice with several 'grossly impertinent' terms of abuse added to the order. He did not leave town, but went to lodge with his friends, the Webers, who had moved to Vienna. After a further stormy interview with his master, Mozart sent in his resignation. It was ignored. After an interval he wrote out his application for a discharge once more, and presented it in person on 8th June. For answer he was kicked out of the Archbishop's house by Count Arco, the high steward. Smarting from this insult, Wolfgang wrote to his father: 'No more Salzburg for me! I hate the Archbishop almost to fury.' He further threatened that, if he met Count Arco in the street, he would return the assault with interest.

Reading between the lines of Wolfgang's letters, it is not difficult to see that, besides his indignation at his treatment by 'this man of God,' he had other motives, when he seized the opportunity to gain his freedom. He clearly hoped to make a career in Vienna and even urged his father to cut himself free from Salzburg and join him in the capital. And there were the Webers. Wolfgang, having lost Aloysia, fell in love with her next sister, Constanze, a plain girl eight years younger than himself. When he realised the position, Leopold, who had a poor opinion of the Webers, was horrified, but Wolfgang knew what he wanted and this time was determined to get it, with his father's consent if possible; otherwise, without it. To Leopold's letters, which put the worst construction on his conduct, he replied with a dignity that only a cynic could dismiss as insincere. Indeed, in view of Constanze's subsequent series of annual confinements, there is, at least, negative evidence that she was not Wolfgang's mistress at this time. Their first child, Raimund Leopold, was born nine months after their wedding on 4th August, 1782.

Wolfgang could, indeed, be as prudish as his father, and during the engagement he took Constanze to task for allowing her leg to be measured during a game of forfeits. Although Wolfgang compares her favourably with the once-adored Aloysia, Constanze had something of her elder sister's capriciousness and love of pleasure. Coming from what we may call a 'Bohemian' household where nothing was ever in order, she was hardly the person to manage the affairs of a young man who had never been allowed by his father any responsibility in money-matters and had persistently been shielded from the practical difficulties of life. Leopold had good cause to be anxious about his son's marriage, but he cannot be absolved from all blame for its disastrous consequences. He had educated Wolfgang admirably as a musician, but he had wholly neglected to prepare him to face life as a man.

The Freemason

The newly married couple were happy enough at the start. They were undoubtedly deeply in love and, if we want a picture of them settling into their home, the first scene in 'The Marriage of Figaro' is probably as truthful a portrait as we could find. In spite of the success of his German comic opera, 'Die Entführung aus dem Serail,' produced in July, 1782, which was patronised by the Emperor, Wolfgang had practically no income and the expected appointment at Court failed to materialise. Within six months they were already in difficulties and Constanze was pregnant. In judging her as a housewife, we must not forget that, for the greater part of her married life, Constanze was either pregnant or recovering from the difficult births of her children, of

whom only two survived, one to become an official in the
Austrian service at Milan and the other an insignificant
conductor and pianist.

There is no reason to suppose that Constanze encouraged
her husband in his work or appreciated his genius—at least
until after his death, when she developed for his music in
retrospect a sentiment never manifested in his lifetime. In
spite, therefore, of his happy companionship with his wife,
Mozart suffered from the loneliness that is possibly the in-
variable lot of great men. It may be that this personal
loneliness—and in this connection Haydn and Beethoven
come to mind—is one of the driving forces that compel an
artist to create.

As a wedding-present for Constanze and as an act of piety
Mozart set to work on the composition of a large-scale Mass
in C minor, but he failed to complete it. He was always
temperamentally incapable of writing without the stimulus
of a definite performance in view, but in this instance a
profound change in his religious convictions made it impossible for him to complete the work. Hitherto Mozart
had shown a childlike faith in religion; but in Vienna he
came into contact with a number of musicians and literary
men who belonged to the secret Society of Freemasons. In
Germany and Austria, Freemasonry had not the exclusively
charitable objects which characterise it in England to-day.
It had political implications that made it as suspect to the
authorities as liberal ideas are to the rulers of modern Germany
and Italy. It gained the accession, however, of men like
Frederick the Great, Goethe and Herder, while in Austria
the Emperor Joseph joined the Society, whose leader in Vienna
was Ignaz von Born. Although, therefore, Freemasonry
was driven underground by oppressive measures and the
disapproval of the Roman Catholic Church, which has
never tolerated secret societies, it was a potent force in
Vienna at this time. Wolfgang persuaded his father to join
the Society, and hereafter his letters are full of cryptic allu-
sions to Masonic ideas. Among other musicians, Gluck

and, surprisingly, that good churchman, Joseph Haydn, were Freemasons.

The year of Mozart's marriage (1782) was prolific in compositions, the most important being the set of six quartets dedicated to Haydn. For a livelihood he took pupils, a task always distasteful to him, and supplied them with music to play. After the birth of their first child, the couple paid a visit to Salzburg in the hope that Leopold might be reconciled to the marriage. Constanze failed to remove the deep-seated prejudices of her father-in-law, which were shared by Nannerl. The visit was uncomfortable and the parting cold.

On returning to Vienna, Wolfgang proceeded to give concerts at the Augarten, with meagre financial results but with great artistic success. Gluck praised his music and the Emperor stayed 'to the very end until the encores were finished.' When it is remembered that these programmes included the 'Haffner' symphony and a series of pianoforte concertos played by the composer, it is easy to share Haydn's indignation at the failure of the Court to recognise his worth by finding him some employment. It was not until the end of 1787, after he had written 'The Marriage of Figaro' and 'Don Giovanni,' that he was appointed chamber-musician and Court-composer to the Emperor with a salary that barely paid his rent.

Several minor operatic projects were occupying Mozart's mind at this time, but they came to nothing. Then, as the result of an amateur performance of 'Idomeneo,' he was brought into contact with an ideal collaborator. Lorenzo da Ponte was an Italian Jew by birth, a priest by profession and a poet by inclination. After a series of adventures not unworthy of Casanova himself—if we may believe the autobiography he published in his old age—he arrived in Vienna in 1783 and wrote librettos for Salieri and Martin. Mozart suggested that da Ponte should adapt for him Beaumarchais' 'Les Noces de Figaro.' This play had been banned in Vienna, and its predecessor, 'Le Barbier de Seville,' had just been successfully staged as an opera with music by Paisiello. There was, therefore, a double incentive for the choice. Da Ponte approached the Emperor and obtained permission for the production of the opera, from whose libretto the more biting passages of Beaumarchais' satire were removed.

'Figaro' was produced on 1st May, 1786, after many difficulties and intrigues. Michael Kelly, the English tenor who created the parts of Basilio and Curzio, records that Mozart was 'as touchy as gunpowder and swore he would put the score in the fire' if his work were not produced before that of the rival, who was trying to forestall him. The opera was most favourably received by the audience, while, after Figaro's air at the end of Act I, singers and orchestra combined with the spectators to acclaim the composer. 'I shall never forget,' writes Kelly, 'his little animated countenance when lighted up with the glowing rays of genius; it is as impossible to describe as it would be to paint sunbeams.'

Yet still nothing was done for Mozart in Vienna. But from Prague, where 'Figaro' was given with immense success, came a commission for a new opera, for which he was to receive 100 ducats. So it was in Prague and not in Vienna that his greatest Italian opera, 'Don Giovanni,' was produced in October, 1787. Da Ponte again provided him with an excellent libretto and the opera achieved a triumphant success.

In the meantime, Leopold, who had come to Vienna for the production of 'Figaro' and joyfully witnessed the fulfil- ment of his most extravagant hopes, fell ill. In spite of the coldness of their relations at the time of his marriage, Wolf- gang's affection for his father had never faltered and their common interest in Freemasonry had drawn them closer together during these last years. He wrote to his father:

'. . . . I need not tell you with what anxiety I await better news from yourself. I count upon that with certainty, although I am wont in all things to anticipate the worst. Since death (take my words literally) is the true goal of our lives, I have made myself so well acquainted during the past two years with this true and best friend of mankind that the idea of it no longer holds any terror for me, but rather much that is tranquil and comforting. And I thank God that He has granted me the good fortune to obtain the opportunity (you understand my meaning) of regarding death as the key to our true happiness. I never lie down in bed without considering that, young as I am, perhaps I may on the morrow be no more. Yet not one of those who know me could say that I am morose or melancholy, and for this I thank my Creator daily and wish heartily that the same happiness may be given to my fellow men. . . . I clearly explained my way of looking at the matter on the occasion of the death of my very dear, my best friend, Count von Hatzfeld. He was just 31, like myself. I do not grieve for him—but from the bottom of my heart for myself and for all who knew him as well as I.'

Herein stand revealed Mozart's mature philosophy and the innate nobility of his mind. Beneath the gay frivolity of his nature, which is so charmingly displayed in his letters to his sister and his wife, there lay a fundamentally serious attitude toward the broad issues of moral conduct and religion in the widest sense. The apparent paradox of his character—the combination of the strictest intellectual discipline, that alone could have produced the perfect union of form and feeling in his music, with a complete lack of discipline in practical affairs—is resolved if we regard it as the sign of a sense of proportion which perceived, more clearly than most of us do, the true essentials of our life. There is no real opposition between his music and his life. Both were ruled by this same sense of proportion, and although it entailed a disregard for all those petty affairs which occupy so much time in the life of the average man, and which are always irksome to men, in Wordsworth's phrase, 'of more than ordinary organic sensibility,' there is never a suggestion of meanness or pusillanimity in his conduct. No sensitive ear can fail to perceive the workings of this mind, at once so deeply emotional and so well-controlled, in the two string quintets, which he wrote after his father's death in May, 1787, or in 'The Magic Flute,' which contains in its fantastic pantomime his whole philosophy of love and death.

The Last Years

The disadvantages of Mozart's philosophy, combined with Constanze's equal incapacity for the practical management of money, are only too plainly to be seen in the following year (1788). It is, indeed, impossible to approach this final phase of Mozart's career without something like a personal sense of sorrow. The story has, apart from its sordidness, every element of tragedy. The catastrophe, inescapable and yet not inevitable, overwhelms the hero owing to a flaw in his essentially fine character. There is even the touch of irony in the offers of help that came just too late to save him, and of supernatural horror in the queer story of the Requiem Mass.

The letters of this period include a number addressed to Michael Puchberg, a rich Viennese merchant, an amateur of music and a fellow Freemason. In them Mozart asks for loans in language that grows ever more pitiable in its despairing appeal. Puchberg was generous, but he could not entirely support the Mozart family. Yet when financial worries were most acute, Mozart was able to write within the space of two months the three symphonies in E flat, G minor and C major, which are his highest achievements in that form. The speed with which he composed is astonishing, but it is well to remember that his was a mind that could think out a whole movement and retain it until the time came to commit it on paper. Herein lies the explanation of the legend that the overture to 'Don Giovanni' was composed on the night before its first performance.

In May of this year 'Don Giovanni' was given in Vienna, but failed to please the audience. The Emperor thought it 'divine, but not meat for my Viennese,' to which Mozart retorted: 'We must give them time to chew it.'

Disappointment and neglect discouraged him and his output fell off. The period of virtuosity was over, and, although he was still to write some of his finest pianoforte concertos, music no longer poured out in such abundance. In his capacity as Court-composer, he wrote, indeed, a quantity of dance-music, for which he received a salary of £80— 'Too much for what I produce; too little for what I could produce.'

In 1789 there was a diversion. He accompanied Prince Lichnowsky on a visit to Berlin. On the way he played before the Court at Dresden, and at Leipzig he seized the chance of enlarging his knowledge of Bach. King Frederick William II received him favourably, commissioned some quartets, for which he received 100 Friedrichs d'or, and offered him, it is said, the post of Kapellmeister with a salary of about £600. It is difficult to believe that he refused such an offer out of loyalty to the Emperor and the Viennese, who had done so little for him, and the story is probably apocryphal. To his wife he wrote, 'You must be glad to have *me* back, and not think of money.' The tour did nothing to alleviate his financial position and its musical outcome was negligible.

Doctor's bills were now added to his other liabilities, for Constanze fell ill and had to go to Baden for a cure. A successful revival of 'Figaro' brought him a commission for another opera, and for the third time he collaborated with da Ponte. 'Cosi fan tutte' was produced in January, 1790, but the illness and death of the Emperor interrupted its career. On the accession of the new Emperor, Leopold II, Mozart applied for the post of Kapellmeister and was refused. Later, in May, 1791, he was appointed assistant, with the right of succession to the post, 'without pay for the present.' But before the office fell vacant he was dead.

The coronation of the Emperor at Frankfurt seemed to offer the chance of making money, but, in order to get there, Mozart had to pledge such valuables as he possessed and borrow money at usurious rates. Characteristically he paid also for the expenses of Hofer, the violinist who had married Josepha Weber, and agreed to share with his brother-in-law any profits that might accrue from the tour. Mozart was ever willing to give away his last shilling to a friend who seemed in need, and his generosity was sometimes shamefully abused. We do not know what money he made during this tour to Frankfurt, where two new pianoforte concertos were produced, but it is improbable that it did more than cover the expenses and the interest on the loan.

The year 1790 had been barren and at its end Mozart's situation was desperate. Yet he declined an offer to go to England. He had been considering such a visit for many years past and, when Kelly, Nancy Storace and his pupil, Attwood, left Vienna after the production of 'Figaro,' he had asked them to arrange matters for him in London. His refusal of a not unreasonable offer is only explicable on the grounds of his own ill-health and Constanze's. Perhaps he felt too weary to seize this opportunity which might well have saved his life. It was Haydn who went to London and made a fortune. Da Ponte, too, had left Vienna, in disgrace, and, having married an Englishwoman, went to London. It is tantalising to imagine what the two might have added as an operatic counterpart to the glory of Haydn's 'London' Symphonies.

Although Mozart was ill, worn out with anxiety, undernourishment and the strain of hard work since childhood, he was soon producing music again with astonishing fertility. Nothing could be more false than the suggestion, sometimes made, that, when he died, he had exhausted his genius. It was his body that gave out, not his mind. There was still plenty of pure metal in the mine that produced during this last year the two strong quintets in D major and E flat, the pianoforte concerto in B flat, and 'The Magic Flute.'

It was in March, 1791, that he received the commission to compose what was to be his last and most imaginative opera. Schickaneder, the author of the libretto, ranks with da

Ponte as one of the most remarkable men with whom Mozart came in contact. An impresario and a comic actor, he was the creator, in every sense of the word, of Papageno. Mozart had met him and composed music for one of his plays years before in Salzburg. Now Schickaneder, who knew his man, lodged Mozart near his theatre on Prince Stahremberg's estate, and set him to work on writing music for the most curious pantomime ever offered to a great composer. In a summer-house in the garden Mozart by some magic transmuted this childish fairy-tale into one of the eternal allegories of man's ideal endeavour. He put into it all his most profound religious convictions, all his sense of 'the mystery of things.' It is the very counterpart in music of 'Everyman' and 'Faust.' Here in the garden Mozart spent his last happy days, perhaps the happiest of all his life.

Work on 'The Magic Flute' was interrupted by a command from the Emperor to write a serious opera for the coronation festivities at Prague. Hurriedly written against time to a frigid classical libretto in a now old-fashioned style, Mozart's imagination was not fired by 'La Clemenza di Tito.' Like all he wrote, it was a piece of good craftsmanship, but not one of his masterpieces.

At the very moment of his departure for Prague in September, there occurred an incident that was to have a profound effect upon Mozart. He had been asked by a mysterious stranger, 'dressed from head to foot in grey,' to compose for a patron, whose identity he must not seek to discover, a Requiem Mass. Now, as he entered his carriage, the stranger, whose manner and costume gave him every appearance of weirdness, had come to demand the fulfilment of the contract. Mozart had been unable to write the Mass and promised to do so on his return to Vienna, but the vision of this stranger took on in his fancy a supernatural aspect, which so affected him that he came to believe that his visitant was none other than the messenger of Death.

That Mozart was at this time in an extremely despondent state is proved by a letter, written apparently to da Ponte, just after this incident. It seems that da Ponte had urged Mozart to come to England.

'I wish I could follow your advice, but how can I do so? I feel stunned, I reason with difficulty, and cannot get rid of the vision of this unknown man. I see him perpetually; he entreats me, he presses me, and impatiently demands the work. I go on writing, because composition tires me less than resting. Otherwise I have nothing more to fear. I know from what I suffer that the hour is come; I am at the point of death; I have come to an end before having had the enjoyment of my talent.'

By how little he missed his enjoyment! 'The Magic Flute' was enormously successful and established at a stroke the future of German opera. A group of Hungarian nobles and admirers in Holland were independently setting in motion schemes to provide him by subscription with a stable income. But it was all too late. He had come to an end, and was unable even to make good his determination, expressed at the end of the letter just quoted, to complete his 'death-song,' the commission for which was a terrible, though unintended, practical joke played upon him by an eccentric nobleman who had lost his wife and desired to commemorate her worthily.

In November his exhausted body began to give way completely and his mind was affected. He imagined himself poisoned by Salieri. At the end of the month he took to his bed, and there, watch in hand, followed in imagination the triumphal progress of 'The Magic Flute.' He worked spasmodically at the Requiem, giving directions to his pupil, Süssmayer, who eventually completed the score. On 4th December, after singing the first strain of the 'Lacrymosa,' he burst into tears and soon lapsed into unconsciousness. Music, the mainspring of his life, was the last faculty left to him, and still as he lay dying he continued to puff out his cheeks as though sounding the trumpets.

Early next morning he was dead and in a few weeks'

time no one knew where his body lay. Constanze was prostrated with grief and unable to attend the funeral. A few friends gathered at St. Stephen's Church for the brief service, but not one faced the bitter cold to follow the greatest composer of his time to a pauper's grave. Very lonely he was in life, and lonely in death, but his spirit lives in the companionship of all who love his music. Alas! for Mozart; alas! for us: he had indeed come to an end before having had enjoyment of his genius.

BIBLIOGRAPHY

CURZON, H. DE: *Mozart*. (Paris, 1914.)

DENT, EDWARD J.: *Mozart's Operas*. 12s. 6d. (Chatto & Windus, 1913.)

HOLMES, EDWARD: *Life of Mozart*. 2s. (Dent, 'Everyman's Library,' 1912.)

HUSSEY, DYNELEY: *Wolfgang Amade Mozart, a Critical Biography*. 3s. 6d. (Kegan Paul, 1928.)

JAHN, OTTO: *W. A. Mozart*. Revised by HERMAN ABERT. 2 vols. (Leipzig, 1923–4.)

JAHN, OTTO: *Life of Mozart*. Translated by PAULINE D. TOWNSEND. 3 vols. O.P. (Novello, 1882.)

Letters of W. A. Mozart. Selected and edited by HANS MERS-MANN. Translated by M. M. BOZMAN. 10s. 6d. (Dent, 1928.)

SITWELL, SACHEVERELL: *Mozart*. 5s. (Peter Davies, 1932.)

SCHURIG, ARTUR: *Wolfgang Amadeus Mozart*. 2 vols. (Leipzig, 1923.)

WYZEWA, T. DE, et SAINT-FOIX, G. DE: *W. A. Mozart, sa Vie Musicale et son Œuvre de l'Enfance à la Pleine Maturité* (1756–1777). 2 vols. (Paris, 1912.)

GIOVANNI PIERLUIGI
DA PALESTRINA

BORN 1525-26   DIED 1594

By Richard Runciman Terry

Prelude—The Man and the Music

I must begin by confessing that I have not made an intensive study of books about Palestrina, but his complete works (in thirty-three volumes) were my daily bread during a choir-mastership of some thirty years. If I add that during that period I was able to perform more of his music than any fellow conductor, it is not by way of a pointless boast, but in grateful and humble acknowledgment of a unique privilege that good fortune happened to throw in my way.

When one thus lives with any given composer over a period of years, week in and week out (as I lived with Palestrina and Byrd), it would be strange if one failed to catch something more of their character and their inmost spirit than the most intensive study of the printed score can furnish. One's deductions can be (and sometimes are) wrong ones, but there is this to be said for constant repetition and constant exploration *in performance*, as opposed to study from the score alone, that it does supply different material for such deductions. The difference seems to me to be something like the difference between a sight of the sea from the cliffs and the experience of sailing upon its waters. The watcher on the cliffs looks upon the same sea with its ever-changing beauty, but his reactions are not the same as the seaman's. The watcher sees its surface: the seaman is enfolded in its embrace; is absorbed into its being; plumbs its depths; penetrates its soul.

High-flown comparisons, you will say? Perhaps so. But I am sure no musician will apply the epithet to the analogy I draw from them. The *reader* of a polyphonic* score is more or less in the position of him who looks seaward from his cliff; the *performer*, the mariner who explores its depths and penetrates its secrets. (I say 'polyphonic' score because a modern one does not quite fit the analogy. The varying timbre of the orchestral combinations—to give but one example—is alone sufficient to keep the æsthetic sense alert and withdraw attention from the disposition and placing of the mere notes. In reading a polyphonic score without this added stimulus the attention is apt to concentrate on the skilful disposition of the *notes*. The modern score yields an æsthetic thrill; the polyphonic one a more or less academic satisfaction.)

I realised something of all this when I first began performing Palestrina's music. As the years went on, the truth of it came home with overwhelming force. I had begun in the usual way, by studying Palestrinian scores until I acquired the erroneous belief that I knew something about Palestrina. I approached my task from the choirmaster's standpoint of previous experience—when the rendering of a piece of church music meant that the choir, so to speak, 'took the stage' while ministers and congregation stood or sat quiescent until the singers had finished. I was gradually to learn that music such as Palestrina composed was but a background to something else which 'took the stage.' Unlike that of Mozart or Beethoven (supremely beautiful though it is *as music*) it was not something imported into the service from outside. It was not music which hampered the orderly progression of the ritual acts. It was not music in which the individuality of the composer dominated the ceremonial by focusing attention on itself rather than on the rite as a whole.

* I use the term in its accepted technical application to unaccompanied vocal (and modal) music of the sixteenth century.

What, then, was the secret of Palestrina's supremacy as a Church composer? It lies much deeper than his supremacy as a musician. The reason why he remains—as truly to-day as in the sixteenth century—the ideal composer for the Roman rite is that he was steeped in the spirit of the Liturgy. His was the larger vision of the liturgist as opposed to the rubrician. The difference between the two is the difference between the artist and the draughtsman. The draughtsman must be a man of skill, but his skill is *acquired*. The artist must be a draughtsman, but to his skill he adds something innate and not to be acquired. The rubrician is a man of book-learning who makes no mistakes; the liturgist's unerring instinct derives from a habit of mind, a cast of character, an individual and comprehensive outlook. When to the inherent 'rightness' of the liturgist is added the gift of music, the result is the Church composer as distinct from the composer (however distinguished) who writes music for the Church. If the art of composition is rightly defined as self-expression in terms of music, then we may say that Palestrina was—of set purpose—expressing in terms of music something he felt to be greater than himself—the mysteries of the faith that was his, as symbolised in the pageantry of rite and ceremonial.

In this respect his music is an index to his character and gives to his everyday life the absorbing interest it has held through four centuries.

The Unknown Teacher

Giovanni Pierluigi took his surname of Palestrina from the Cathedral town of that name, twenty miles from Rome, where he was born. The old Latin name of the city was Præneste and in his Latin dedications, and other writings, Palestrina signed himself (Johannes Petraloysius) Prænestinus, under which name his compositions appear in 'Proske' and other collections, to the sore bewilderment of non-linguistic choirmasters.

The actual year of his birth remained for long in doubt, but it has now been fixed, with fair certainty, at 1525/6. Modern research has also disposed of the presumptive poverty of his parents. They were not people of rank, but they owned considerable property in houses and land.

Great men are seldom infant prodigies who command, in consequence, a good Press before adolescence. The early years of Palestrina are unrecorded until we hear of him in 1537 as one of the choirboys in the cathedral of his native town. There is great uncertainty as to his early instructor, or instructors, in music. A writer of the seventeenth century gave his tutor's name as Gaudio Mel, adding that he was a Flemish musician of much talent. From this arose the conjecture that the person indicated was Goudimel. Against this supposition we have the statement by some modern authorities that Goudimel was never in Rome, but the late Dr. G. R. Woodward used to give strong reasons for the Goudimel supposition. Some other writers have identified Gaudio Mel with one Firmin le Bel who was appointed choirmaster at Palestrina Cathedral in 1540, but the probabilities are against such identity. The possibility of Arcadelt as Giovanni's early instructor 'has its points,' but all we can say nowadays is that the evidence—one way or the other—is conflicting and that, after all, it does not really matter. We do know that the boy Giovanni did 'return to Rome for study' in 1540. As the Papal Choir always had the services of the first musicians in Europe, the boy was therefore sure of the best instruction.

He was recalled to his native city in 1544 'to play the organ on festivals' and to sing daily in the cathedral choir at Mass, Vespers and Compline, with the additional duties of instructing both canons and choirboys. The revenues of a canonry were set aside as his remuneration. It seems so obvious to the modern reader that the person in charge of cathedral music should play the organ that he may well inquire why this stress on playing it 'on festivals.' The answer is that the services on festivals would be pontifical functions that would involve additional ceremonial with its consequent waits. These gaps were, as they still are, filled in by music on the organ until the celebrant was ready to continue the Liturgy. 'Supplying' is the term now used to describe the duty.

Marriage and Rome

At twenty-one years of age Palestrina married and we hear little else of him until, three years later (1550), the Bishop of Palestrina was elected Pope, taking the title of Julius III. This was an important event for the composer, for Julius called him to Rome in the following year to take charge of what was known as the Julian Choir, a choral body attached to the Pope's person, founded by Julius II as a training ground for Italian singers to feed the Sistine Choir. The Sistine Choir (*Cappella Sistina*) is frequently confounded with that of St. Peter's, but they are two distinct bodies, the latter attached to the Basilica of St. Peter and the former to the person of the Pope, in the same way that the English Chapel Royal was attached to the person of the Sovereign—moving about with him and at his disposal whenever required. It has been supposed, possibly with some truth, that the dilution of the Papal Choir with Italian singers from the Julian foundation was to lessen the predominance of foreigners in the former body.

Palestrina published his first volume of Masses in 1554 and—doubtless as a tribute of gratitude to his benefactor—dedicated it to Pope Julius. A modern writer has noted the fact that, since the first Mass in the book is entitled 'Ecce Sacerdos Magnus,' the publication was a piece of flattery addressed to the Sovereign Pontiff. Surely (if the Mass in question had any bearing on the point) here was a mere act of courtesy, since the Pope *was* 'Sacerdos magnus,' being officially—in title as in fact— 'Pontifex maximus.' To most people the explanation is a simpler one. The Mass in question has for its *canto fermo* the melody of the antiphon *Ecce sacerdos magnus* and that seemingly is 'all there is to it.' If I mention this Mass at all, it is because it has significant historical bearing. It not only employs the melody of *Ecce sacerdos*, but, whenever that melody occurs in the course of the composition, the words of the *antiphon*—not the words of the Mass—are placed underneath it, a course of procedure that, as will appear later, composers were eventually forbidden to adopt.

In 1555 the Pope—by special command—appointed Palestrina to the post of singer in the pontifical choir (the *Sistina*). This appointment was resented by the members of that very close corporation on several grounds, the chief being that the status made membership dependent upon examination and approval of the candidate by the whole college of Beckmessers. This was in January; in March of the same year Julius III died, and in April his successor was elected, taking the title of Marcellus II. He died three weeks after election, but his reign claims our notice from the fact that he is the Marcellus in whose honour Palestrina wrote his immortal 'Missa Papæ Marcelli'—not published, however, until twelve years later.

The next Pope, Paul IV, was a reformer. Amongst other affairs, he took in hand the discipline of the Papal Chapel. Three members were dismissed with a pension, in accordance with the statute requiring the singers to be single men. Palestrina was one; another was Domenico Ferrabosco, father of the Alfonso Ferrabosco who settled in England and became to all intents and purposes an English composer.

Choirmaster at the Lateran

In the October of 1555, however, Palestrina obtained the appointment of choirmaster at the Basilica of St. John Lateran—an important post then (as now), since the Lateran is the cathedral church of the Pope in his local capacity as Bishop of Rome. The next three years at the Lateran were fruitful as regards Palestrina's compositions. They included his book of 35 Magnificats and his Lamentations for four and eight voices. They are settings of those texts from the Prophet Jeremiah's lamentations that form part of the office of *Tenebræ* in Holy Week. One modern writer comments on the fact that Palestrina sets only two or three verses for each 'Lection' compiled from the prophet for liturgical use. But this was quite in conformity with rubrical authority. As a complete setting of every verse to elaborate music would have inordinately lengthened the service, it was sufficient if a single chorister recited, *submissa voce*, the verses that the composer omitted. To this same period, 1555–8, belongs a work—which even if it stood alone would have secured Palestrina's reputation for all time—the 'Improperia' (Reproaches), which occur in the Mass of Good Friday. This composition attracted the notice of the formidable Paul IV, who seemed, from that time onward, to appreciate the genius of the musician whom he had formerly dismissed from office. He had the music copied into the books of the Sistine Choir—the first composition of Palestrina to receive that honour. Henceforward it was heard every Holy Week in the Sistine Chapel until the ceremonies there were suspended in 1870. Mendelssohn's *Letters from Italy* give some idea of its appeal to musicians of every generation and every country.

The year 1558 marked Palestrina's sudden resignation of his Lateran post. Most authorities have it that he became dissatisfied with increasingly onerous conditions imposed by a cathedral Chapter that did not appreciate the genius of its *maestro*. The Pope—now his friend—does not seem to have been able to do much for him, but in 1561 we find Palestrina installed at another basilica—St. Maria Maggiore —at a salary of £156 per annum, which—together with his own private property and the 'gifts' usual on festivals or other important occasions—would seem to indicate the comfortable circumstances that presumably favoured the composition and publication of the important works belonging to that time.

The Council of Trent

In 1562 occurred an event—the summoning of the Council of Trent—which was to have an intimate bearing on the work of Palestrina and every other Church composer. Musical histories are responsible for the general impression that the Council of Trent was a musical affair. In actual fact, music played a very small part in its deliberations. But, briefly, it did consider, amongst other matters, the abuses that had crept into musical settings of the Liturgy. One of these was the extent to which composers had used tunes with secular associations as the *canti fermi* of their Masses. The question was entirely one of decorum, edification of the faithful, and of expediency as to the methods of proposed reforms. Musical text-books give harrowing accounts of the 'irreverence' that could incorporate secular tunes into the music of a Mass, to the disedification of the congregation. This is sheer exaggeration. First the Council of Trent (as ecclesiastical authority had done before, and has constantly done since) 'took stock,' amongst a multitude of weightier matters, of the existing state of ecclesiastical music and made such regulations as they deemed desirable for the fulfilment of its *raison d'être*, namely, the adornment of the Liturgy. That was all. Secondly, it is worth remembering that when secular tunes were used as *canti fermi* the notes were turned into a procession of *breves*, each breve usually occupying a whole bar of the music. It would require a listener of more than average intelligence to detect a melody moving at this snail's pace, in equal notes (which deprived it of its rhythm), and embedded in a maze of swiftly moving counterpoint. Thirdly, even when, on the rarest of occasions, the 'tune' was on the top—as in the English Masses on the song 'Western Wynde'—with some semblance of its original rhythm, he must be a strange species of critic who can describe the effect as 'irreverent.'

One result of the Council's deliberations was the eventual recognition of Palestrina as a supreme model in the matter of polyphonic settings of the Liturgy. The proposal of certain members of the Council that every kind of music save the Plainsong should be swept away met with no real support.

Cardinal d'Este—The Masses

The year 1569 sees Palestrina in the services of Cardinal d'Este, one of the outstanding figures of the Renaissance. High-born and wealthy, he was nevertheless a man of wide culture and a liberal patron of the arts. He owned beautiful palaces, the one in Rome being noted for its collection of ancient Greek and Roman sculptures; he also maintained a private choir. He gave every encouragement to Palestrina and the result appears in the number and importance of his compositions during this period. To it belongs the publication of two books of Masses which include the famous 'Missa Papæ Marcelli'; the delightful 'Missa Inviolata' (which—by the way—is most effective if transposed down for *men's* voices); the much misrepresented 'Missa Ad Fugam,' described by superficial critics as 'academic' (true it shows a high degree of scholarly ingenuity, but, so far from its proving 'dry' to my own choir, it became one of the favourites); the 'Missa Sine Nomine' for six voices that has proved so intriguing to some conscientious critics. (These patient students have shown perturbation at their non-discovery of any 'theme' in the 'Sine Nomine' Masses. No wonder. The title 'Sine Nomine' was usually applied to Masses *not* founded on any particular *canto fermo*.) To this period also belong the famous 'Missa Brevis,' the much be-written 'Miss Ut Re Mi' and the equally talked-about 'Missa L'Homme arme'—all three published in 1570. In spite of its name, the first is not a 'short' Mass; '*brevis*' here does not refer to relative length; more possibly it indicates the measure of the *Tactus*, which in this case is a breve. The second (on the notes, *Do, Re, Mi, Fa, Sol, La*) is anything but academic. It contains more 'block harmony' than Palestrina usually employs in six-part work, but the *Kyrie* is beautifully fluent; so is the *Agnus Dei*, while the *Sanctus* is almost a riot of brilliancy. The third has suffered much from various types of exponents. The purists are stern about its use of a 'secular' tune; the text-books tell us how skilfully the composer juggles with the mysteries of 'Proportions,' and finally, Dr. Haberl (in the complete edition of Palestrina's works) disregards the composer's unequivocal time-signatures in his transcription of it. In reality it is a good, singable Mass, all the better because it leaves the listener unconscious of its fearsome contrapuntal dexterity.

The Music

This is not a critical essay on Palestrina's music, but a few running comments may be permissible at this stage. First, one is impressed by the liturgical fitness of his compositions; his 'Offertoria,' for example, never hold up the Mass by their undue length; even his eight-part 'Stabat Mater' does not unduly delay the service to which it belongs. His Masses fit every liturgical occasion, from the *Feria* up to the elaborate *Festa* or the lengthy ceremonial of a pontifical function. Secondly, his clefs, unlike those of English polyphonists, always indicate a definite type of voice beyond whose range he never goes. He makes no daring experiments (as does Byrd); hence the gratefulness of his music to the singer. Thirdly, none of these self-imposed limitations affect the æsthetic appeal of his music. He can achieve perfection in a short motet like 'Bone Pastor' and can reach the topmost peaks of awe and grandeur with simple, plain chords, as witness his 'Improperia' and 'Stabat Mater.'

Like Byrd, he left no setting of the *Te Deum*, and he never wrote a complete 'Requiem.' Neither did he compose a 'Passion.' In fact, the more one studies his works the more illuminating does one find them (especially in their omissions) as a running commentary on the Rome of his day. Just one example: I once expressed—to a liturgical authority

—my surprise that Palestrina, so intimately associated with Popes, had not written an 'Ecce Sacerdos.'* I received the answer that the Roman custom is to greet a Pope on his entry into the church with 'Tu es Petrus' instead.

Palestrina did not write music at random. His compositions are, in such ways as I have mentioned, in the nature of guide-posts for us who follow his career.

The Man

In addition to that of Cardinal d'Este he enjoyed the patronage and friendship of William, Duke of Mantua. Much of their correspondence has been preserved, and if it shows the Duke as an enlightened patron of the arts, it brings out the more intimate side of Palestrina and the old text rises to one's lips, 'Behold an Israelite indeed, in whom there is no guile.' In mundane affairs Palestrina lacked Byrd's grip and driving force, but both men were alike in their serene detachment from them. Each lived an interior life, hence the poise and balance of their exterior. Palestrina suffered much at the hands of jealous colleagues—the small fry of the *Sistina*—but amongst the *composers* of his day he enjoyed the same reverence and affection which Byrd inspired in his contemporaries. Asola (no mean composer himself) sums up their attitude when he says that Palestrina was 'the ocean towards which all streams flow.'

In such a full, rich life as his, one can do no more, in this short sketch, than pick out the salient points that have a bearing on his own character or upon subsequent history. His intimate friendships with St. Charles Borromeo and St. Philip Neri are cases in point. When we have dismissed the legends about Palestrina's musical contributions to the 'Oratorios' at St. Philip's *Chiesa Nuova*—his 'Madrigali Spirituali' (the 'Canticle of Canticles') may have been

---

* I do not forget the 'Ecce Sacerdos' included in his 'Doubtful Works.' That volume seems the correct place for it.

F

preformed to the cultured congregations who assembled there, but he certainly wrote no 'Laude Spirituali' as did his predecessor Animuccia—there is no reason for disbelieving Baini's account of the last days of the composer or his touching tribute to S. Filippo's affectionate service of the *maestro* to the end.   In the light of recent research we are a little inclined to underrate Baini as an authority.   He certainly does go astray on historical points, but that does not lessen his credibility when he deals with matters of tradition.   We are apt to forget that Baini was a man of considerable learning and wide culture, with a scholar's appreciation of Palestrina and his music.   It has become the fashion to treat him as a sort of garrulous Boswell.   But do not let us forget that, writing in 1828, he had the disqualification of being a Boswell without his Johnson.

The 'Graduale' and its Lesson

One incident in Palestrina's career cannot be passed over, as its far-reaching effects have lasted into our own times.   One of the results of the reform of the Missal and Breviary under Pius V was a general desire that the Plainsong, the *official* music of the Church as distinct from that which anyone was at liberty to compose, should be reclaimed from the corruption into which it had fallen.   In 1576–7 Gregory XIII issued the necessary order for its revision and the task was allotted to Palestrina and Zoilo (his successor at the Lateran). Palestrina undertook that portion of the 'Graduale' known as 'The Proper of the Season' and Zoilo the portion entitled 'The Proper of the Saints.'   After working hard at this task, Palestrina suddenly abandoned it in 1578 when it was near completion.   Many reasons have been assigned for his action.   After examining them all I am of opinion that— artist as he was—Palestrina realised the hopelessness of ever tracking the melodies, through endless stages of corruption, to their original source.   Clearly no element of pique influenced his decision, for when his pupil Guidetti, in his private capacity, issued *his* revision of the 'Directorium Chori,' Palestrina wrote a commendatory preface.

Then comes the sequel to all this. After Palestrina's death, his son Iginio managed to extract from a private printing press (the 'Medicean') the promise of a large sum of money if he obtained official approval of the revised 'Graduale,' in which case they would print it. Iginio seems to have obtained every sort of approval save an official one. His shiftiness during the 'deal' brought on an indecisive lawsuit. Iginio died in 1610 and the printers again took up the matter, entrusting the revision of the MS. to Felice Anerio and Soriano. No one seems to know whether they eventually tendered Palestrina's MS. or their own, but as it conformed with the notions of Plainsong then current amongst musicians, it was published in 1614 with more or less general approval but still no official sanction. This 'Medicean Edition,' as it was called, eventually fell into desuetude. In the sixties of last century there was a strong revival of the liturgical spirit in Germany. A society for the reform of liturgical music was initiated and its influence soon became a factor to be reckoned with. It eventually turned its attention to the reform of Plainsong, by that time almost chaotic in its variations, and conceived the idea of republishing the Medicean Edition of 1614 on the ground that it was Palestrina's work. With an astute publisher behind them, they managed to secure a thirty years' monopoly of the printing of it for the Holy See. It was edited by Dr. F. X. Haberl of Regensburg and is known as the Ratisbon Edition. Under the aegis of Palestrina's name the Ratisbon party claimed it as the Church's Chant restored to its original purity. The exposure of its errors by subsequent research did not prevent their putting the clock back for thirty years (for their monopoly 'scotched' the efforts of other reformers at Rheims, Cambrai, Malines and elsewhere) until Pius X, in 1903, undertook the reform of Plainsong in real earnest and appointed a commission of experts to prepare the present *Editio Vaticana* which rejected medieval accretions and went back to the only true source—the texts of original MSS. —a thing that Palestrina had not been able to do. In the light of these events, Palestrina's abandonment of the 'Graduale' assumes a different aspect from that presented by musical histories. I cannot attribute his action either to a sudden freak or to pressure of other work. It seems to me that, as his work on the 'Graduale' progressed, he began to realise the true nature of the texts upon which he had to work. All available ones were more or less corrupt. The very existence of the original MSS. was forgotten. At the bottom of his artistic soul he realised that he had embarked on a hopeless task. His clear artistic vision revealed to him in 1578 something which the rest of the world did not discover until 300 years later.

It is this fundamental 'rightness' that characterises Palestrina and gives him unchallenged right to the title with which his contemporaries invested him—*Princeps Musicæ*. His personal rectitude is reflected in his music with its crystal clarity and singleness of aim. If we keep that in view we shall see how everything he wrote falls into place as part of one great scheme. His fertility was amazing, as the thirty-three volumes of his known works testifies. Yet amongst the ninety-five Masses, nearly 400 motets and an almost equal amount of other music, it would be difficult to lay a finger on any single one and say it gave evidence of being thrown off in the mood of the moment. He did not write capriciously or at haphazard. From his great works—such as the 'Stabat Mater,' the Masses 'Ecce Ego Joannes' or 'Dum Complerentur' down to his smallest motet—we see but one aim, the presentation of the liturgical ideal and the subordination of everything else in life to that end.

BIBLIOGRAPHY

Brenet, Michel: *Palestrina.* (Paris, 1906.)
Casimiri, Raffaele: *Il a codice 59, dell'archivio musicale lateranense.* (Rome, 1923.)

CASIMIRI, RAFFAELE: *Firmin le Bel de Noyon*. (Rome, 1922.)
CASIMIRI, RAFFAELE: *Memorie musicale prenestine.* (Rome, 1924.)
MOLITOR, RAPH: *Zur Vorgeschichte des Medicaea*. (Freiburg, 1899.)
PYNE, ZOË KENDRICK: *Giovanni Pierluigi da Palestrina; his Life and Times.* O.P. (Lane, 1922.)
RAUGEL, FÉLIX: *Palestrina.* (Paris, 1930.)
  N.B.—Raugel gives a copious bibliography.
RESPIGHI, C.: *Palestrina e l'emendazione del Graduale romano.* (Rome, 1899.)
WAGNER, PETER: *Palestrina als weltlicher Komponist.* (Strassburg, 1890.)

HENRY PURCELL

BORN 1658   DIED 20 November 1695

By Ralph Hill

Charles II and his Court

On 3rd September, 1658, Oliver Cromwell anticipated
Beethoven by dying during a terrific storm. The Common-
wealth was ended and the power of the Puritans broken.
In 1660 Charles II succeeded to the throne and there came
about an inevitable reaction against the rigours of the Puritan
mode of life. Cynicism and profligacy became fashionable;
Charles and his Court emulated the luxurious living of the
French king, Louis XIV. Evelyn describes how he saw in
the royal palace 'the new fabric of French tapestry, for design,
tenderness of work, and incomparable imitation of the best
paintings beyond anything I had ever beheld. Some pieces
had Versailles, St. Germain's, and other palaces of the French
king, with huntings, figures and landscapes, exotic fowls, and
all to the life rarely done. Then for Japan cabinets, screens,
pendule clocks, great vases of wrought plate, table-stands,
chimney furniture, sconces, branches, brasenas, etc., all of
massy silver, and out of number, besides some of her majesty's
best paintings.' Evelyn gives a picture of the scene at Court
six days before Charles's death: 'I can never forget the in-
expressible luxury, and profaneness, gaming, and all dis-
soluteness, and, as it were, total forgetfulness of God (it
being Sunday evening), which this day se'nnight I was witness
of: the king sitting and toying with his concubines, Ports-
mouth, Cleveland, and Mazarine, etc.; a French boy singing
love-songs in that glorious gallery, whilst about twenty of
the great courtiers and other dissolute persons were at basset

round a large table, a bank of at least £2,000 in gold before them; upon which two gentlemen who were with me made reflections with astonishment.'

In 1662 a theatre in Lincoln's Inn Fields was opened, and in the following year another appeared in Drury Lane. In 1671 there was built in Dorset Gardens, near the Temple, another, which specialised in elaborate and spectacular musical productions, such as a version of Shakespeare's *Macbeth* with appropriate incidental music. But in the name of 'entertainment' many liberties were taken with Shakespeare, or whoever the author happened to be. New characters were introduced, cuts were made in order to make way for remarkable transformation scenes that smacked of magic and mystery, and songs and dances were added to increase the appeal. In Shakespearian productions a tradition was begun that found its apotheosis in Sir H. Beerbohm Tree's productions at His Majesty's Theatre before the last war.

Early Days

Among such conditions Henry Purcell, one of England's greatest composers, was born, it is said, in 1658, at a house in St. Anne's Lane, Old Pye Street, Westminster. Little is known about the origin of his family and hardly more about his life, which is wrapped in obscurity. Purcell's father, also named Henry, held several important posts as a professional musician. He was a Gentleman of the Chapel Royal and sang in the choir at Charles II's coronation. He was also a member of the Royal Band and sang at Westminster Abbey, where he was choirmaster and music copyist, the latter an important position in view of the fairly wholesale destruction of church music during the Puritan regime. Pepys records in his diary on 21st February, 1659, that, 'after dinner, I went back to Westminster Hall with him [Mr. Crewe] in his coach. Here I met with Mr. Lock and Pursell, Masters of Musique, and went with them to the Coffee House, into a room next the water, by ourselves, where we spent an hour or two. . . .   Here we had a variety of brave Italian and Span-ish songs, and a canon for eight voices, which Mr. Lock had lately made. . . .'

Purcell appears to have received his first musical instruction from his father at about the tender age of four or five, but on 11th August, 1664, Purcell's father died, leaving his son to the care of his brother, Thomas Purcell. Two years previ-ously Thomas Purcell had succeeded Henry Lawes as Musician in Ordinary 'for the lute and voyce', for which services he was allowed 'the wages and living of six-and-thirty pounds two shillings and sixpence by the year during his life.' No doubt through his uncle's influence Purcell now became a chorister in the Chapel Royal, where he remained until his voice broke in his 15th year. Purcell studied under Matthew Locke and Captain Henry Cooke, who was Master of the Children. According to Pepys, Cooke was a vain coxcomb who sang uncommonly well. In 1672 Cooke resigned 'by reason of sicknesse' and Pelham Humfrey took his place.

Humfrey at the age of seventeen had been sent to Paris by Charles II to learn the French style of composition from the famous composer Lully. Pepys describes him as follows: 'Little Pelham Humphreys lately returned from France, and is an absolute Monsieur, as full of form and confidence and vanity, and disparages everything and everybody's skill but his own. But to hear how he laughs at all the King's musick here, at Blagrave and others, that they cannot keep time or tune, nor understand anything: and at Grebus, the Frenchman, the King's Master of Musick, how he understands nothing, nor can play any instrument, and so cannot compose: and that he will give him a lift out of his place, and that he and the King are mighty great.' Purcell does not appear to have been influenced by Humfrey's French predilections. In 1673 Purcell, the 'late child of his Majesty's Chapell Royal, whose voice is changed, and gon from the Chapell' was given £30 a year together with fine holland, handkerchiefs, a felt hat and (later) 'one and twenty ells, three quarters of holland, and four whole shirts, four half shirts and four bands and cuffs' in return for duties as 'keeper, maker, mender, repayrer and tuner of the regalls, organs, virginalls, flutes and recorders and all other kind of wind instruments whatsoever, in ordinary, without fee, to his Majesty, and assistant to John Hingston, and upon the death or other avoydance of the latter, to come in ordinary with fee.' In the following year Humfrey died and his post was taken by Dr. John Blow, whose pupil Purcell became.

Copyist and Composer

Two years later Purcell was appointed music copyist at Westminster Abbey, which duties he carried out until 1678. Meanwhile he had already several compositions to his credit, among which was an ode for the King's birthday—'The Address of the Children of the Chapel Royal to the King, and their Master, Captain Cooke, on his Majesties Birthday, A.D. 1670, composed by Master Purcell, one of the Children of the said Chapel.' In 1676 Purcell composed music for three plays, Shadwell's *Epsom-Wells* and *Libertine* and Dryden's *Aurenge-Zebe*.

In 1677, Matthew Locke, one of the great founders of English opera, died and Purcell was made Composer in Ordinary for the Violin. He also composed an 'Elegy' in memory of Locke. In 1680 Dr. Blow resigned so that, it is believed, Purcell could succeed to his post as organist of Westminster Abbey. During the same year Purcell composed his famous opera 'Dido and Æneas' for a girls' school in Chelsea. The original copy of the libretto bears the following inscription: 'An Opera performed at Mr. Josias Priest's Boarding-school at Chelsey, by young gentlewomen, the words made by Mr. Nat. Tate. The Musick composed by Mr. Henry Purcell.' This opera is one of the landmarks of English music and is generally considered to be one of the composer's outstanding achievements. Purcell now appears to have been making a good enough living to get married, for about this time he married Frances Peters, who belonged to a well-known family in the parish of St. Margaret's, Westminster.

The year 1682 was eventful. Purcell was appointed organist of the Chapel Royal, his uncle Thomas, who had done so much for him, died, and his first son, John Baptista, was born; three more sons and a daughter followed at intervals. Furthermore, he composed the music for 'The inauguration of the truly loyal and right honourable Sir William Pritchard, Knight, lord Mayor of the City of London, president of the honourable Artillery Company, and a member of the worshipful company of Merchant-Taylors. Performed on Monday, September XXX. 1682.' The next year saw Purcell as one of the King's Composers, and as a direct consequence he published a set of 'Sonnatas in III Parts' for two violins and bass and bearing a dedication to the King. An advertisement appeared in the *London Gazette* pointing out that 'These are to give Notice to all Gentlemen that have subscribed to the Proposals Published by Mr. Henry Purcell for the Printing his Sonatas of three Parts for two Violins and Base to the Harpsecord or Organ, that the said Books are now completely finished, and shall be delivered to them upon the 11th June next: and if any who have not yet Subscribed, shall before that time Subscribe, according to the said Proposals (which is Ten Shillings the whole Sett), which are at Mr. Hall's house in Norfolk-street, or at Mr Playford's and Mr. Carr's shop in the Temple; for the said Books will not after that time be Sold under 15s. the Sett.'

Music and Medicine

Playford was the leading publisher of the time. In one of his publications there appeared a delightful advertisement concerning his business activities: 'At Mr. Playford's shop is sold all sorts of ruled paper for musick and books of all sizes ready bound for musick. Also the excellent cordial called 'Elixir Proprietatis,' a few drops of which drank in a glass of sack or other liquors is admirable for all coughs, consumption of the lungs, and inward distempers of the body; a book of the manner of taking it is given to all those who buy same. Also if a person desires to be furnished with good new Virginals and Harpsicons, if they send to Mr. Playford's shop they may be furnished at reasonable rates to their content.'

Characteristic of Purcell's modesty and an interesting insight to his attitude towards French and Italian music is the preface to the set of 'Sonnatas in III Parts,' which runs: 'Ingenious Reader. Instead of an elaborate harangue on the beauty and the charms of Musick which (after all the learned Encomions that words can contrive) commends itself best by the performances of a skilful hand, and an angelical voice: I shall say but a very few things by way of Preface, concerning the following Book, and its Author: for its Author, he has faithfully endeavoured a just imitation of the most fam'd Italian Masters; principally, to bring the Seriousness and gravity of that sort of Musick into vogue and reputation among our Country-men, whose humour, 'tis time now, should begin to loath the levity and balladry of our neighbours. The attempt he confesses to be bold and daring, there being Pens and Artists of more eminent abilities, much better qualified for the imployment than his, or himself, which he well hopes these his weak endeavours, will in due time provoke, and enflame to a more accurate undertaking. He is not asham'd to own his unskilfulness in Italian Language; but that the unhappiness of his Education, which cannot justly be accounted his fault, however he thinks he may warrantably affirm, that he is not mistaken in the power of the Italian Notes, or elegency of their Compositions, which he would recommend to the English Artists. There has been neither care, nor industry wanting, as well in contriving, as revising the whole Work; which had been abroad in the world much sooner, but that he has now thought fit to cause the whole Thorough Bass to be Engraven, which was a thing quite beside his first Resolutions. It remains only that the English Practitioner be enform'd, that he will find a few terms of

Art perhaps unusual to him, the chief of which are these following: *Adagio* and *Grave* which imports nothing but a very slow movement: *Presto*, *Largo* and *Vivace*, a very brisk, swift, or fast movement: *Piano*, soft. The Author has no more to add, but his hearty wishes, that his Book may fall into no other hands but theirs who carry Musical Souls about them; for he is willing to flatter himself into a belief, that with Such his labours will seem neither unpleasant, nor unprofitable. Vale.'

At the end of the year 1683 Purcell was appointed 'keeper, maker, repairer and mender and tuner of all and every his Majesty's musicall wind instruments; that is to say all regalls, virginalls, organs, flutes, recorders and all other kind of wind instruments whatsoever, in the place of John Hingston, deceased.' His salary was £60 in addition to any expenses incurred in the execution of his duties.

Friendship with Dryden

In 1685 Charles II died and James II ascended the throne, but three years later James fled and in the following year William and Mary were crowned at Westminster Abbey to the strains of Purcell's organ. Apart from his executive work Purcell was turning out a great deal of composition, much of which was connected with the theatre, such as the music for *The Tempest*, *The Massacre of Paris*, *The Prophetess or the History of Dioclesian* (Beaumont and Fletcher), and Dryden's *Amphitryon*. Dryden's interest in Purcell was awakened when he heard the music for *Dioclesian*; in consequence they became great friends and collaborated in several dramatic works. In his dedication to *Amphitryon* Dryden says: 'What has been wanting on my part has been abundantly supplied by the Excellent Composition of Mr. *Purcell*; in whose Person we have at length found an *Englishman* equal with the best abroad. At least my Opinion of him has been such, since his happy and judicious Performances in the late Opera, and the Experiences I have had of him, in the setting of my three

Songs for this *Amphitryon*: To all which, and particularly to the Composition of the *Pastoral Dialogue*, the numerous Quire of Fair Ladies gave just an Applause on the Third Day.'

Purcell followed this up with the music to Dryden's *King Arthur*, which is one of Purcell's most ambitious dramatic works. Dryden prefixed to the text a note in which he said that 'There is nothing better, than what I intended, than the Musick; which has since arriv'd to a greater perfection in England, than ever formerly; especially passing through the artful hands of Mr. *Purcell*, who has compos'd it with so great a genius, that he has nothing to fear but an ignorant, ill-judging audience. But the numbers of poetry and vocal musick are sometimes so contrary, that in many places I have been oblig'd to cramp my verses and make them rugged to the hearer: of which I have no reason to repent me, because these sorts of Entertainments are principally design'd for the ear and the eye; and therefore, in reason, my art on this occasion ought to be subservient to his.'

Late Hours and Merry Company?

In a house on the west side of Dean's Yard, Westminster, Purcell died in the presence of his wife and family on November 20th, 1695. On the same morning Purcell had made his Will, which ran: 'I Henry Purcell of the Citty of Westminster gent., being dangerously ill as to the constitution of my body but in good and perfect mind and memory (thanks be to God) doe by these presents publish and declare this to be my last Will and Testament And I doe hereby give and bequeath unto my loveing wife ffrances Purcell all my Estate both reall and personall of what nature & kind soever to her and to her Assignes for ever And I doe hereby constitute and appoint my said loveing wife my sole Executrix of this my last Will and Testament revokeing all former Will or Wills.' Purcell was buried in the north aisle of Westminster Abbey 'in a magnificent manner.' The chief cause of his death was undoubtedly consumption, but Sir John Hawkins, the old historian, gives credence to the story that circulated during the eighteenth century to the effect that Purcell died 'by a cold which he caught in the night waiting for admittance to his own house.' It is said that he was in the habit of keeping late hours and merry company and on one night, 'heated with wine from the tavern at an hour later than prescribed him,' his wife had the doors bolted against him. Whatever the reason, England lost one of her greatest musicians, who promised even more than he had achieved.

BIBLIOGRAPHY

ARUNDELL, DENNIS: *Henry Purcell*.   3s. 6d.   (Oxford University Press, 1927.)

CUMMINGS, W. H.: *Purcell*.   O.P.   (Low, 1903.)

HOLLAND, A. K.: *Henry Purcell; The English Musical Tradition*. 6s.   (Bell, 1933.)

WESTRUP, J. A.: *Purcell*.   5s. 6d.   (Dent, 'The Master Musicians' Series, 1937.)

ALESSANDRO AND GIUSEPPE DOMENICO SCARLATTI

Alessandro: BORN 1659   DIED 24 October 1725
Domenico: BORN 26 October 1685   DIED 1757

By Frank Howes

The Scarlatti Family—Background

Like the Purcells, the Couperins and the Bachs, the Scarlattis were a family of musicians. Like the Wesleys, father and son attained an approximately equal eminence in their own generation. Contemporary or rather post-contemporary opinion, as reflected in the pages of Hawkins and Burney, takes it as a matter of course that Alessandro was the greater man and his son merely a brilliant and much travelled virtuoso performer who had composed a good deal of music for his instrument. Posterity, though quite content to take the assurance of scholars that Alessandro laid the foundations of classical harmony for the subsequent use of the Viennese masters, rarely hears a note of his music, but finds the vitality of Domenico's sonatas undiminished. Alessandro may live in history; Domenico is one of the composers who still minister to our daily needs.

The family came from Sicily, and in official documents Alessandro described himself as 'of Palermo.' His father Pietro, of whom little is known, though it is surmised that he too may have been a musician, left Sicily in 1672, and settled in Rome, where Alessandro, now a boy of fourteen, began his musical education. Born in 1659, he was an exact contemporary of Henry Purcell and senior by one year to Bach's predecessor at Leipzig, Johann Kuhnau, who, like Domenico Scarlatti, was to contribute an element to the evolution of keyboard sonatas. Heinrich Schütz, 'the father of German music,' was over seventy when Alessandro Scarlatti first saw the light. François Couperin, the Great French composer, styled 'le Grand' to distinguish him from the rest of his family, who practised music generation after generation, was nearly ten years Scarlatti's junior. These then were his contemporaries, but, since cultural influences mostly flowed from Italy northwards and not at this time in the reverse direction,* they have no bearing on Scarlatti's development; they merely serve to determine his position in the longitude of time. His Italian seniors and contemporaries, on the other hand, helped to mould his style— Stradella (1645–82), Legrenzi (1625–90), Carissimi (1604–74), from whom he may have had lessons during his first year in Rome, and the Venetians, Cesti (1620–69) and Cavalli (1602–76). From Carissimi he derived his sense of key, from Stradella his sense of melody, from the Venetians his sense of form, notably that of the *aria da capo*, and from Legrenzi his principles of construction in cantata and opera—though to put it so is probably to over-crystallise the truth.

Queen Christina

Next to nothing is known of Alessandro's early life. He married a Roman girl when he was barely twenty, in April, 1678, and by this time his father was dead. In 1679 his first opera, 'Gli Equivoci nel Sembiante' (Mistaken Identity), was performed in Rome and was sufficiently successful to win for him the patronage of Queen Christina of Sweden. This remarkable lady, daughter of the great soldier-king,

---

* A reservation must be made about French influence: the Court of Louis XIV was taken as a model all over Europe, and in music the increasing vogue of the French overture is a significant symptom of a more general cultural movement.

Gustavus Adolphus, has always attracted the attention of biographers and historians: biographers because of her sexual inversion, and historians because she abdicated her throne. Modern psychology professes to read the riddle which the politically minded historian has always found insoluble—for historians think in terms of power and do not understand how anybody can voluntarily prefer a good, still less an artistic, life to the possession of power. The circumstances of her upbringing developed the masculine side of her temperament and gave her strong intellectual interests. She ascended the throne at the age of six and began actively to rule the country when she was seventeen. Refusing to marry and so provide an heir to the throne, she abdicated and left herself free to abandon the barbarous life of Sweden and pursue a cultured life in the South. She settled in Rome, which at this time was governed by the Pope, and became prominent in its social life. She had always been a lavish patron of learning; by making Scarlatti her *maestro di cappella* she extended her patronage to art.

Pope Alexander had welcomed the Queen to Rome as a royal convert from Lutheranism to Catholicism, but the Queen was an embarrassing resident, and, although she had abandoned high politics, she retained enough regal imperiousness to take a hand in the aristocratic manœuvres for local influence, prestige and dispensation of favours. Scarlatti had a sister, Anna Maria, an opera singer who was secretly married to an ecclesiastical personage—or perhaps not so secretly, since contemporary account says that Scarlatti was in bad odour at the Vatican on account of this sister. On one occasion at any rate, it came to blows between the Pope's Swiss guard, who were doing police duty at the doors, and the lackeys of Cardinal Colonna, who was in attendance on Queen Christina as the Pope's representative, for the Queen had sent for Scarlatti that he might play in the orchestra at one of the repeat performances of his opera. The guard had refused to open the door to the Cardinal, but Queen, Cardinal and musician together forced an entry. Five years later Scarlatti, having by then gone to Naples, still describes himself (in the libretto of his opera 'Pompeo') as *maestro di cappella* to the Queen of Sweden.

Naples and Rome

Either in 1682 or in 1684 Alessandro transferred himself to Naples, where he probably had family connections, for his father when taking him on to Rome as a small boy had left his two youngest brothers at Naples, and Naples was henceforth to be the family home of the Scarlattis and to become in virtue of that fact the seat of a 'school' of composers. 'Pompeo' was first given in Rome in 1683, but it was repeated at Naples in the spring of 1684, and just as 'Gli Equivoci' had secured him an appointment with the Queen of Sweden so the later opera secured for him the post of *maestro di cappella* to the Viceroy of Naples (at that time a Spanish possession) and a post as violinist in the orchestra for his younger brother, Francesco. In the next year (1685) his son Domenico was born on October 26th. While his family was growing up he remained at Naples turning out operas, cantatas and chamber music for aristocratic consumption.

By 1702, however, he had become dissatisfied. The political troubles, which five years later culminated in the wresting of Naples from Spain by Austria after two hundred years of continuous possession, were working up and made conditions bad for the exercise of music. Alessandro, therefore, without resigning his official position, applied to the Viceroy for leave of absence for himself and Domenico and betook himself to Florence to see whether he could find employment with the Grand Duke Ferdinand de Medici. He avoided Rome, because operatic production was difficult owing to the opposition of the reigning Pope, Innocent XII, for though less severe than Innocent XI, who had closed the theatre, he followed the Vatican tradition of opposition to the stage as subversive of public morality.*   Ferdinand, on the other hand, was an enthusiastic musician with a private theatre attached to his palace, and commissioned several works from Scarlatti for it.   But he offered him no permanent appointment—finding his style somewhat severe for his own taste—although the two men remained friends and exchanged a voluminous correspondence with each other on artistic subjects.   Alessandro was therefore driven back on Rome, where he was offered a poor appointment as assistant director of music at the church of S. Maria Maggiore, for he was determined not to return to Naples, where at last, on 25th October, 1704, his post was declared vacant.   Although he put up with his Roman church appointment for himself, he was not satisfied to keep Domenico in Rome; in the following spring he sent him off to Florence with a letter of introduction to Duke Ferdinand, explaining that Naples did not offer the right opportunities for Domenico's particular talents, which were not of the operatic sort required there, but were by now making him conspicuous as a virtuoso of the harpsichord, and that Rome offered 'no roof to shelter Music, which lives here in beggary.'

Alessandro owed his appointment in Rome to the good offices of Cardinal Ottoboni, whose family had taken an interest in his work at least a dozen years before.   General Ottoboni, the Cardinal's father, visiting Naples in 1694, made a point of seeing the new opera 'Pirro e Demetrio,' which incidentally was to find its way to London in the early years of the Italian opera at the Haymarket (in 1708).   Ottoboni made Alessandro his own *maestro di cappella* in 1707, and for him Alessandro wrote many of his cantatas.   Opera production in Rome was still practically impossible, so that Scarlatti was forced to find a use for his operas elsewhere, notably with Duke Ferdinand at Florence and at Venice,

* In 1697 Innocent XII ordered the destruction of the Tordinona Theatre which had been rebuilt earlier in his reign, and performances were also forbidden at the Capranica Theatre.

whither he went to produce 'Mitridate Eupatore,' his most
ambitious effort so far. He returned, however, to his
ecclesiastical duties in Rome for Christmas. 'Lucio Manlio,'
which he sent to Ferdinand in the summer of 1705, he
declared to be the eighty-eighth dramatic work he had
composed in a period of twenty-three years. Of his total
output thirty-five now survive.

The Arcadian Academy

Money was one of Scarlatti's troubles at this period of his
life, but honours were beginning to come to him. In 1706
he was elected along with Corelli, the founder of violin
playing, and Pasquini, the organist of St. Mary's, a member
of the Arcadian Academy. This fantastic institution was one
of Queen Christina's creations. All through her restless life
she poured her surplus energies, which were great even when
she had taken her fair share in the social and political intrigue
of the time, into scholarship, ranging from philosophy to
chemistry and the arts. Immediately on her arrival in Rome
in 1656 she founded the *Academia Reale* and twenty years
later she refounded it as the Clementine Academy, which
met at her palace for the discussion of literary, political and
psychological problems. On her death in 1689 the Academy
became homeless and had to meet wherever it could obtain
hospitality among the Roman grandees. On a fine day in
1692 its members, littérateurs, lawyers and pedants, met in
the open air and were so worked upon by the beauty of the
scene and their own eloquence as to cause one of them to
exclaim that Arcadia was re-establishing itself among them,
whereupon they all went pastoral and rechristened themselves
with the names of Arcadian shepherds. This little affectation
invested the Academy with all the fascinations of a secret
society and it became fashionable. When Scarlatti was
admitted he adopted the name of Terpandro Politeio.
Hitherto musicians had been professionally engaged for the
concerts of the academies, which had by this time spread

through Italy in imitation of the Roman model. These three were the first musicians to be elected to academic honours.

Domenico and Handel

Meantime Domenico, described by his father in the letter to Ferdinand as 'an eagle whose wings are grown,' went on from Florence to Venice under the escort of Nicolini. Nicolini was one of the greatest operatic singers of his day; he earned golden opinions for his dramatic abilities as well as for his singing. Burney describes him as 'the first truly great singer who had ever sung in our theatre.' Leaving Domenico in Venice, where he studied with Gasparini and met Handel, Nicolini came on to London and duly appeared in the performance of Scarlatti's 'Pirro e Demetrio' already mentioned. It is quite possible that Handel met both Scarlattis in Venice at the time of the production of 'Mitridate Eupatore.' Mainwaring says that it was at Cardinal Ottoboni's that Handel met Alessandro. But as his chronology is vague we cannot be sure of the precise order of events. Mainwaring (*Recollections of Handel*, p. 59) writes: 'When he [that is, Handel] first came into Italy the masters in greatest esteem were Alessandro Scarlatti, Gasparini and Lotti. The first of these he became acquainted with at Cardinal Ottoboni's. Here also he became known to Domenico Scarlatti now living in Spain [he was wrong here, whether "now" means 1708, the date of the episode he is about to describe, or 1760, the date of his book, when Domenico was already dead] and author of the celebrated "Lessons." As he was an exquisite player on the harpsichord the Cardinal resolved to bring him and Handel together for a trial of skill. The issue of the trial on the harpsichord has been differently reported. It has been said that some gave the preference to Scarlatti. However, when they came to the organ there was not the least pretence for doubting to which of them it belonged. Scarlatti himself declared the superiority of his antagonist and owned ingenuously that till he had heard him upon this instrument he had no conception of its powers.' According to another story, however, Domenico recognised Handel by his playing at a masquerade in Venice before this. He had heard of Handel's achievements in Rome, and when at this party in Venice a masked stranger played so astonishingly, Domenico exclaimed that it must either be 'the Saxon' or the devil. At any rate the two men became firm friends, so much so as to cause Mainwaring to say that Domenico 'followed him all over Italy and was never so happy as when he was with him,' adding that Handel reciprocated these feelings, as he 'used often to speak of this person with great satisfaction—for besides his great talents as an artist he had the sweetest temper and the genteelest behaviour.'

Alessandro, Corelli and Gasparini

In 1709 Domenico entered the service of the Queen of Poland in Rome and Alessandro returned to Naples, which had now become an Austrian possession. The Austrian Viceroy tried to get him back, though at first he could offer him no more than the deputy-organistship of his establishment, but he was ultimately able to offer Alessandro his old post as director of music by persuading its occupant to stand down in his favour. The appointment was specially confirmed by the next Viceroy, Count Daun, and he settled down for a second time in Naples and began to produce operas on a big scale. He was now in his fifties, enjoying a great reputation and finding full exercise for his powers in opera, oratorio, symphony, cantata and church music. His career was outwardly crowned in 1716 by the honour of knighthood, conferred possibly in acknowledgment of an opera composed to celebrate the birth of the Archduke Leopold.

To this period of Alessandro Scarlatti's life belong two anecdotes of his dealings with brother musicians. In 1708 Arcangelo Corelli, the great violist and founder of modern violin playing, visited Naples, which Scarlatti and his orchestra had by now made the musical capital of Italy.

Corelli was a simple soul who had already had his feathers ruffled in an encounter with Handel in Rome, though his reputation there had stood high from former days when the Queen of Sweden gave her concerts. He wished to make a good impression in Naples and took with him three of his own instrumentalists, but he found the Neapolitan players equal to all the demands of his music; not so himself to the music of Scarlatti, for he started off in C major a piece in C minor, so that Scarlatti, who was conducting, had to suggest that they should start again. The hint, however, was not enough and to his great humiliation Corelli had to be put right by Scarlatti, whose tact had been unavailing. Scarlatti was five years his junior, but they were fellow Academicians and probably understood each other quite well. The other story also shows Alessandro as an extremely efficient and friendly person. Burney relates that the elder Scarlatti had a great regard for Gasparini, 'then a composer and harpsichord master of great eminence'—so much so that he 'placed his son Domenico, while a youth, to study under him in that city' (Venice). In 1712 the two made an exchange of compositions rather in the manner of Byrd and Ferrabosco, who a century before had engaged 'in a vertuous contention in love betwixt themselves made upon the plainsong *Miserere*,' or of Brahms and Joachim, whose practice it was at one time to exchange weekly contrapuntal exercises. Gasparini sent to Scarlatti a cantata called 'Andate o miei sospiri' (Go, O my sighs), to which Scarlatti replied with two more settings of the same text, one comparatively simple and expressive, the other full of abstruse technical contrivances. The first he said was *in idea humana*, the second 'inhuman' setting was 'in the chromatic style not for every professor,' and its chromaticism was, and was meant to be, startling. The solution of technical problems has a natural appeal to the musician as to the mathematician, and it is interesting to find Scarlatti in company with Byrd, with Bach (in his 'Musical

Offering' and his 'Art of Fugue') and with Brahms, revelling in sheer musical skill.

Domenico Travels

Domenico at this time was living in Rome, occupied in composing operas for the Queen of Poland's private theatre and church music for St. Peter's, to which he was appointed choirmaster in 1715. A couple of years later Alessandro was also in Rome. But there seems to have been a little friction between father and son when Domenico, now thirty-two years old, sought to obtain his full legal status and be free of his father's control, in preparation for the life abroad he was now to begin. First he went to London (1719) and stayed for the production of his opera 'Narciso' at the Italian Opera in the Haymarket in the following May, twelve years after his father's first production on a London stage. His uncle Francesco was in London at the same time and gave a concert consisting largely of his own works a month or two later, for which he made the most of his connection with the great Alessandro and the brilliant visitor. In the next year Domenico went off to Lisbon and took service with the King of Portugal as Court musician and teacher of the Infanta Maria Magdalena Barbara of Braganza. He did not, however, remain there for many years, since in 1725, the year of his father's death, we find him back in Naples. We have it on the first-hand authority of Hasse, the popular German composer of operas, that Domenico got back home before his father died. Dr. Burney, travelling over Europe in the latter part of the century to collect material for his history of music, encountered Hasse in Italy and asked him whether he had ever heard Domenico Scarlatti play the harpsichord. To which Hasse replied that he had, 'as he [i.e. Domenico] came from Portugal to Naples on a visit to his father while he [i.e. Hasse] studied under him [i.e. Alessandro].' 'He allowed him to have been possessed of a wonderful hand, as well as fecundity of invention'—is Burney's report of Hasse's judgment.

Alessandro's End

The last years of Alessandro's life were divided between Naples and Rome. In October 1717 he repeated the proceedings of fifteen years before and got leave to go to Rome to produce his last and greatest operas. He retained his post at Naples but did not draw the salary. Operas of his continued to be produced in Naples, including his one comic opera 'Il Trionfo del Onore,' and doubtless he went to and fro for their *premières*. He also busied himself with a dozen orchestral symphonies begun in 1715, but he must have given up his teaching. He had been appointed to the staffs of three of the four conservatorios of Naples—choir-schools originally founded for the education of orphans and by this time the nursery of many famous composers. He also published a treatise on playing from figured-bass, *Regole per Principianti* (Rules for Beginners). This is virtually a text-book of harmony, but being aimed at keyboard performance rather than at exercises in composition it places the emphasis less on rigid rules than on what sounds well. Herein he is the father of his son, for Domenico always laid great stress on the appeal of music being to the ear: 'To my thinking,' he says, 'there is no other rule in music worthy of a man of genius than to please that sense the delight of which is the sole object of music.'

The last we hear of Alessandro is from Quantz, the famous German flautist, who taught the flute to Frederick the Great and met Bach on a famous occasion at the Court of Potsdam. 'In 1725,' Burney informs us, 'Quantz went to Naples, where he met his countryman Hasse, who then studied under Alessandro Scarlatti. . . . Quantz entreated Hasse to introduce him to his master, Scarlatti, to which he readily consented; but upon mentioning him to the old composer, he said "My son, you know I hate wind instruments, they are never in tune." However Hasse did not cease importuning him till he had obtained the permission he required.' The meeting must have been a success, for Scarlatti composed a couple of flute solos for Quantz. A few months later he was dead.

The details of the latter part of Domenico's career are curiously scanty. He lived in Spain for a quarter of a century, and it was thought for a long time that he had died there, but a Naples musical paper of 1838 declares that he returned home in 1754 and spent the last three of his seventy-two years in the city of his birth. 1754 is the year in which the Queen of Spain died. She was none other than his old pupil, the Infanta Barbara, who had married the Prince of Asturias. In 1729, when her marriage took her from Lisbon to Madrid, she sent for Domenico to come and continue her lessons with him. For her he wrote the pieces which were published under the name of 'Lessons.' He himself only published one collection of thirty 'Exercises,' but his Anglo-Irish friend Thomas Roseingrave superintended the publication of others in London. The King of Spain was the melancholy Philip V, who died in 1746. When the Prince of Asturias ascended the throne as Ferdinand VI he retained Scarlatti's services, that he might play to the Queen in the evenings, and gave him a Court pension. Farinelli the singer, another Neapolitan, was also a Court musician at Madrid at the time, having been employed by Ferdinand's step-mother to sing to Philip nightly the same four songs—which may have been good for Philip's melancholy but was certainly bad for Farinelli's art. Farinelli, however, gained in political power more than he lost in artistic eminence and amassed a fortune into the bargain. His services, too, were retained by Ferdinand till his death in 1754. Farinelli then retired to Italy and settled at Bologna and was thus able to assist Scarlatti's family when Domenico died. For Domenico was a gambler and dissipated his savings so that there was nothing left for his dependents.

Domenico seems to have been an easy-going sort of person without the self-conceit of the virtuoso, but without much strength of character or of physique. His modesty is attested by the story that if anyone in Madrid praised his harpsichord playing, he would reply by invoking the name of Handel and crossing himself in veneration of the great German.

There is also a letter of his extant, addressed to the Duke of
Alba, which reveals a friendly disposition, and Handel, as
we know, bore testimony to his personal charm.   The indica-
tions are that he went downhill in later life.   Burney could
certainly have told more than he did about him, for he says
that Farinelli 'furnished me with all the particulars concerning
Domenico Scarlatti which I desired'; but Farinelli, as we
know, was only too well acquainted with Scarlatti's gambling
propensities and the facts of his last twenty-five years are
to-day shrouded in obscurity owing to Burney's reticence.
There are two pieces of evidence that he was a sick man.
In 1740 he was in Ireland, at the invitation, presumably, of
Thomas Roseingrave, who thirty years before had met
him at Venice and conceived so great a liking for him and
admiration of his musicianship that he followed him
round Italy during the time he was studying there.   Burney
even styles Roseingrave the 'head of the Scarlatti sect,'
and Roseingrave, now living in Dublin, arranged two
benefit concerts for Scarlatti, to which the most prominent
Irish musicians gave their assistance.   *Faulkner's Journal* of
Dublin contains announcements on 3rd and 7th February,
in these terms:

'BY SUBSCRIPTION

'At Johnson's Musick Room in Crow Street, Saturday the 7th
February next, will be performed a Concert of Vocal and Instrumental Musick, for the benefit of Signor Scarlotti [*sic*] who thro'
a long confinement by Sickness is reduced to very distressful
Circumstances.   On this occasion Mr. Dubourg will play a Solo
and Mr. Worsdale will perform some Songs.   Three tickets for
half a guinea.   Single tickets a British Crown.'

London and Domenico's End

To the information contained in this public notice it may
be added that he left Ireland in 1741 for London, where he
remained for a year, during which time he contributed

songs to two pasticcio operas: of these two of the songs
were introduced into 'Alessandro in Persia' by the singers as
their own choice, according to the licence permitted to them
by the operatic convention of the day (in the manner of the
'Lesson' song in 'The Barber of Seville,' though with less
dramatic justification); one was an aria contributed to an
opera 'Merope o l'Olympiade,' composed for the most
part by Pergolesi, and one was an aria that may have been
taken from his own 'Merope,' which was produced in Rome
in 1740.

The other document bearing on Domenico's ill-health
is more personal. The date of the letter to the Duke of
Alba is not certain, but it has been put as late as 1754, and
it was sent with the manuscript of certain hymns that the
Duke had commissioned. It runs as follows:

'YOUR SERENE HIGHNESS:

'It seems good to me that I should stay and await your happy
return here, so that I may express my devotion not only by sending
the enclosed manuscript, but by assuring you of my readiness to
undertake any further commission with which you may honour
me.

'Transcribing the words, which are Latin, but written in Gothic
abbreviations, has given me more trouble than anything else,
which I pray your Excellency to observe; another difficulty was
the old parts which I have scored, not only to do honour to the
great man who is dead, but also in order that from them many of
our modern composers may observe and learn the true rules of
contrapuntal writing—that is to say if they are willing to do so,
for nowadays only a few care for this.

'I cannot go out, and you, Excellency, are strong, noble and
gracious. Why do you not then come to comfort me with a
sight of you? Perhaps I am not worthy of this? True indeed;
but where is the home of virtue if not in the hearts of the great?

'With this I will close. I pray God that He will fulfil your and
my desires and bless you—Amen.

'SCARLATTI.'

His second visit to the British Isles, his letter to the Duke of Alba and his final return to Naples are the last we hear of him, except for one reference in Burney which throws an odd little side-light on his old age.

Burney in Vienna met a certain M. L'Augier, who showed him some of Scarlatti's music with which he was not familiar. 'In Spain,' says Burney, 'he [i.e. L'Augier] was intimately acquainted with Domenico Scarlatti, who, at seventy-three, composed for him a great number of harpsichord lessons which he now possesses, and of which he favoured me with copies. The book contains forty-two pieces, some slow movements—of all these I who have been a collector of Scarlatti's compositions all my life have never seen more than three or four. They were composed in 1756* when Scarlatti was too fat to cross his hands as he used to do, so that these are not so difficult as his more juvenile works which were made for his scholar and patroness the late Queen of Spain, when Princess of Asturias.' L'Augier further reports that Scarlatti had admitted to having 'broken the rules of composition' for the gratification of the ear, and had admitted as well that the music he wrote 'imitated the melody of tunes sung by carriers, muleteers and common people.' 'He used to say,' continues L'Augier, 'that the music of Alberti and several other modern composers did not in the execution want a harpsichord, as it might be equally well, or perhaps better, expressed by any other instrument, but as Nature had given him ten fingers, and as his instrument had employment for them all, he saw no reason why he should not use them.'

Both these Scarlattis are shadowy figures to us living three centuries after them. But although we have fewer facts about Domenico to go on, his personality comes to us with

* M. L'Augier's dates do not tally with the account already given of Domenico's last years, according to which he was no longer in Spain in 1756; and in any case he would be no more than seventy-one in that year, since he died in 1757 at the age of seventy-two.

a sharper imprint than does that of his father, whose doings have been more fully recorded. It is partly, no doubt, from his music that we get the aroma of his personality and partly from such anecdotes as these which Burney has recorded from first-hand sources. Alessandro, the greater man, stands further back in the shadow of time. And so these two lives throw an interesting light on the difference between biography and history.

BIBLIOGRAPHY

DENT, EDWARD J.: *Alessandro Scarlatti; his Life and Works*. O.P. (Arnold, 1905.)

LEE, VERNON: *Studies in Seventeenth-Century Italy*. O.P. (Unwin, 1907.)

SITWELL, SACHEVERELL: *A Background for Domenico Scarlatti; 1685-1757*. 5s. (Faber, 1935.)

PENGUIN OCCASIONALS

PENGUIN FILM REVIEW
Edited by R. K. Neilson Baxter, Roger Manvell and H. H. Wollenberg

Free of any financial ties with the film industry, *Film Review* provides the intelligent film-goer with a survey of the international cinema—as art form, as entertainment, and as a social influence.

PENGUIN MUSIC MAGAZINE
Edited by Ralph Hill

A commentary on music and on musical affairs written, by professionals, for the amateur and the newcomer to music. Among regular features are reports on musical activities in the provinces and overseas, on Opera, Ballet, new music, records, and books.

PENGUIN NEW WRITING
Edited by John Lehmann

A miscellany of critical and creative writing. Its contributors include many of the world's leading writers and artists, but the editor also publishes in his selections much interesting new work by new authors.

SCIENCE NEWS   *Edited by John Enogat*

Current development in scientific research explained by experts in such a way as to be comprehensible and interesting to the layman, and useful to the scientist who wishes to keep up with developments in fields outside his own specialisation.

All one shilling per issue or five shillings for four issues (including postage) from the publishers.

RUSSIAN REVIEW
Edited by Edward Crankshaw

The life, culture, resources and political activities of the U.S.S.R. objectively discussed.

NAVIGATION ON THE ROAD?

When the *Queen Mary* enters a busy port, she and all the other vessels obey the recognized lights and signals on which safe navigation depends.

We, too, obey lights and signals — and rely on them for safety — when we drive or ride or walk on the roads.

We are, in fact, "road navigators." Modern traffic simply could not work without a set of rules which we all accept.

Why, then, are there still accidents — far too many?

Partly because we don't all know and understand the rules and principles of Road Navigation. And even if we know them, we forget or ignore them. And partly because some of us don't yet realize that the rules apply to *everyone* — walkers as well as cyclists and drivers. *Any* of us can cause an accident in which we or other people get killed or maimed.

If we all understood the principles of good Road Navigation (based on the Highway Code) and obeyed them *all the time*, traffic would flow faster and more smoothly. We should all get about more easily and, above all, *more safely*. By learning to be skilful Road Navigators, we can help ourselves and everyone else to *get home safe and sound*.

GET HOME SAFE AND SOUND

Issued by the Ministry of Transport